BILAL AL-HABASHI

BILAL AL-HABASHI

Hilal Kara and Abdullah Kara

NEW JERSEY • LONDON • FRANKFURT • CAIRO • JAKARTA

TUGHRA
BOOKS
New Jersey

Copyright © 2016 by Tughra Books

Originally published in Turkish as *Bilal-i Habeşi* in 2015.

19 18 17 16   1 2 3 4

Published by Tughra Books

345 Clifton Ave., Clifton,

NJ, 07011, USA

www.tughrabooks.com

Library of Congress Cataloging-in-Publication Data Available

ISBN: 978-1-59784-927-2 -

Printed in Canada by Marquis

Contents

CHAPTER 3

CHAPTER 4

CHAPTER 1

PERIOD OF ENSLAVEMENT

THE YEMENITES' CALL FOR HELP

The life story of Bilal al-Habashi, may Allah be well pleased with him, begins with the Najranites living in Yemen appealing to the Abyssinian king for help in the face of Himyarite persecution.

This was close to a century before the rising of the radiant sun of Islam in the skies of the Arabian Peninsula. The Himyarite Kingdom reigning in the south of Yemen was the site of frequent struggles for power and rule changed hands constantly. When Dhu Nuwas came to power and the end of such a struggle, the land turned into a bloodbath. With not a shred of compassion or mercy, Dhu Nuwas descended upon the land like a dark cloud on the day he ascended to the throne. The tyrannous ruler began bloodshed from the moment he became king, leaving no evil that he did not subject the people to. He usurped the property of some and the wealth and possessions of others. He beat those he wished and killed those he wished. He crushed the weak and seized the property of the rich. He persecuted the people to the point of debilitation. The protection of one's life and property could not be spoken of.

His insatiable thirst for power and dominance led his tyranny to increase with each passing day. Himself a polytheist, the king could not bring himself to accept the Najranites' being Christian. He harassed the people living here on a variety of pretexts, persecuting ordinary people struggling to survive, who kept to themselves. He raided their places of worship, insulted and assaulted religious leaders and burnt their sacred scriptures. Those who opposed him, he massacred without mercy.

When this oppression became impossible to endure and innocent people were killed, a committee of wise men came to together in search of a solution. One of them said, "We can appeal to the Abyssinians for help. I do not think that the king who is Christian like us, will remain indifferent to our call for help."

With the committee's acceptance of his proposal, they selected a few people from amongst themselves and these envoys who possessed powerful oratory were ready in a short time. They set off to Abyssinia, on the other side of the Red Sea.

Crossing by boat, they went straight to the king's palace. They sought permission to appear before him. After introducing themselves, they related all the oppression and persecution they face and sought help from the king. They described in tears how their churches had been raided and their holy books burnt. The tears of the king moved by what he heard flowed down his cheek, wetting his beard. When the handed the burned Bibles they had taken with them to the king, everyone was crying.

A deep silence overtook the palace when the envoys concluded their words. The king was deeply grieved by what he had heard. But this was not the reason for his silence. The real cause of the sorrow enveloping his heart and preventing his speech was his inability to do anything to help. When he finally raised his head he said in a sad tone of voice:

"I really want to help you. I have plenty of men, but no ships to transport them across the Red Sea at the same time. If we were to send them in groups, your enemies would kill them at once as soon as they disembarked."

He was right. This was not the answer the envoys expected and this demoralized them. The distress, sadness and sorrow engulfing their hearts projected onto their faces. They appealed to the king once more, saying, "Please find a way of resolving the issue of the ships and save us from this persecution. Otherwise this tyrant will ruthlessly kill even our babies."

Taking pity on them, the king consulted with state officials and decided upon asking for help from the Byzantine emperor. He sent his trusted men as ambassadors to Byzantium. He ordered these ambassadors to take the partially burnt Gospels with them in order to easily persuade the emperor. The messengers set out without delay and went straight to the palace when arriving in Byzantium. They related the situation in the emperor's presence, presenting the burnt sacred scriptures to him at the end of their address. Like the Negus, the emperor too was exceedingly upset by the oppression against his coreligionists. The sight of the burned Gospels was enough to throw him into a rage. He accepted the appeal for help and sent a large number of ships to Abyssinia.

The emperor's positive response to the call greatly pleased the Negus who then formed an army consisting of thousands of men, which he subsequently sent to Yemen to the aid of the Najranites. When Dhu Nuwas became aware of the situation, he hatched a sinister plan instead of facing the advancing army.

He had a large number of keys made and set out to the Red Sea coast taking these with him. Here, he set up camp waiting for the arrival of the ships. He met the army and requested to meet with their Commander. With his request accepted, he said to the Commander, "There is no need for us to fight each other and kill our young. If you promise that you will touch no one and spare our youth, then we will surrender our land to you without any resistance." He handed the keys that he had brought with him to the Commander as a show of earnestness, saying, "Here are the keys to the gates of all the villages, towns and cities of Yemen. Take them and go to the forts where you will be able to take control of them without any resistance."

Oblivious to the sinister plan, the commander accepted the proposal and was delighted that he would take Yemen without a fight. He took the keys and gave them to his troops, dispatching them to all corners of the country to take possession of these forts.

Days passed. Convinced that conditions were ripe Dhu Nuwas progressed to the second phase of his plan. He sent word to his men in every village, town and province, ordering them to, "Slaughter each and every black bull within their land," on a particular day and at a specific time.

The Yemenites receiving the message massacred every Abyssinian they saw at this particular time. Thus was a great army completely destroyed in an instant with a clever plan. None survived except for those few who managed to escape and secretly flee to Abyssinia. Having an audience with the Negus, they related the ambush of the Yemenites and the disaster that befell them. Filled with rage, the ruler of Abyssinia sent against him an army of seventy thousand men under the command of Aryat and Abraha al-Ashram, to Yemen.[1]

---

[1]   Ibn Tahir al-Maqdisi, *Kitab al-Bad' wa't-Tarikh*, 3:184.

INVASION OF YEMEN

When the army reached Yemen, they encountered Dhu Nuwas' army and five times its size, the Abyssinian army overran it in a short time. When Dhu Nuwas realized that he would be killed he rode his horse headlong into the Red Sea and spurred it forth until he vanished and was never seen again.

The Abyssinians won a major victory with the death of Dhu Nuwas and gained full control over Yemen where they established themselves as rulers. The Abyssinians realized that they were here to stay and quickly completed the necessary preparations to settle in the country.

Abraha, one of the leaders of the Abyssinian army, was an ambitious man. He was satisfied with developments and began plotting to set himself up as ruler over Yemen. He provoked disturbance in the army. He then invited Aryat to single combat in way of resolving the matter and deceitfully killed him. Cunningly, he redeemed himself in the eyes of the Abyssinian ruler once more and became king of Yemen. In this way, the set of events which began with the Najranites' call for help led to the collapse of the Himyarite kingdom and to Yemen's colonization. The Yemenites, separate from the people of Najran, never came to accept what had befallen them. But they were helpless. Therefore, they had to resign themselves to the new rulership, even if unwillingly.

Angry at the Yemenites for destroying the first Abyssinian army, Abraha treated them very harshly. He forced them to accept Abyssinian hegemony.

In the second army which came to the aid of the Najranites there was a young soldier by the name of Rabah. This was the first time he left his homeland and set off for distant lands and the first time he had traveled by ship. When he boarded the ship to cross the Red Sea, he was exceedingly nervous and a little scared.

During the trip, he thought constantly of home. His life flashed before his eyes. One thing led to another when they disembarked at Yemen. Before long, they encountered the Yemenite army. He was furious with the men for having slyly destroyed the Abyssinian army not long ago. When the battle began, he threw himself forward to avenge the death of his friends. He had many brushes with death.

The Yemenis were unable to withstand their large forces dispersed in a short time. Some were killed, while others fled and barely escaped with their lives. Rabah was satisfied that they had avenged the death of their fellow countrymen and went to Yemen's capital Sana'a with the rest of the forces. After staying here for some time, he was then commissioned in one of Yemen's districts.

ABRAHA'S AMBITION

Rabah, who was worried when leaving his homeland due to a fear of what his future held, got used to Yemen in time, even liking it. While the Yemenis viewed them as occupying forces, they got used to them as their relations with the people developed.

In fact, everything would have gone right were it not for the ambition of leaders, their efforts at consolidating their positions, and their desire to expand their sphere of dominance. Problems would have been resolved in time and the people would have lived happily in peace. But things do not always go as desired. The greed and ambition of the rulers knew no end. They forever wanted more and more. They lost sight of their actual purpose and instead of using the power they got from the people to serve them; they used it to oppress them.

Abraha had done so also. He had long forgotten that he had come to Yemen to prevent oppression and made plans to dominate the entire Arabian Peninsula. He assumed that he would easily accomplish his objective once he solved a few complications. One of these complications was the Ka'ba, the Sacred House that was visited in throngs by pilgrims from all over the Arabian Peninsula. The Ka'ba ensured the people's solidarity and unity. Abraha first took to reducing the power of the Ka'ba upon the people. To this end, he decided to have a temple built that would bedazzle the Arabs. He supposed that those who saw such a temple would visit this instead of the Ka'ba.

He set to work immediately. Artisans were brought to Sana'a and the finest materials were readied. When preparations were complete, work began for the construction of one of the most beautiful churches in the world. Abraha refrained from no sacrifice in order for the building to be a magnificent one and he had materials procured from all across the globe. An awe-inspiring church was built at the end of great exertion.

The interior walls of the edifice adorned with precious stones brought in from various places were clad in white, black, yellow, and red marble.

Abraha avoided no expense, even sending his men to the place of Balqis, Queen of Sheba, to bring the stones from there.

The interior design of the church was meticulously done. Every quarter was embellished with such precious materials as gold, silver, ruby, emerald, and chrysolite. The door handles and knockers were made of gold. The shrine dazzled with its gilding, workmanship and grandeur and at its completion became one of the world's most important churches.

Hearing of the church's beauty, Rabah himself visited it several times, loving it more each time. He attended mass and soaked up its spiritual atmosphere.

Abraha wanted for the church to be considered a holy site and visited not only by Christians but by all Arabs. This is why he encouraged the Arabs to visit the church. He sent his men to the villages calling the people to visit the site and a lack of interest led him to use force. He did not get the result he had hoped for despite this. Far from diverting the Arabs' interest from the Ka'ba, his attitude only increased it. Faced with such a situation, Abraha set out with a great army to march against the Ka'ba and demolish it.

FROM COMMANDERSHIP TO CAPTIVITY

When Rabah, who served in the army in Yemen, heard of Abraha's setting out to Mecca with a large army, he was very concerned. He did not like the idea of war despite being a solider because irrespective of whoever the victor was, mothers would be left crying, wives widowed and children orphaned.

Anxious and apprehensive, he began waiting for news to come from Mecca. Weeks followed the days and the shocking news finally came. Attempting to destroy the Ka'ba, succumbing to his unbridled ambition, Abraha was subjected to Divine punishment and was destroyed along with his men. He was very upset when he heard the news. He was overcome by immense fear and trepidation. His hopes for the future faded. His gut feeling was right. Nothing in Yemen had ever been the same after that day.

When Abraha died, his son Yaqsum took his place. Yaqsum, who was just as oppressive as his father, died in a short period of time and was succeeded by his brother Masruq. Masruq was merciless and his despotism and persecution made his father look innocent in comparison. He spread unimaginable terror throughout the land, usurping the property, lives and honor of the people. Witnessing all the goings-on was enough to remind Rabah of why they had come to Yemen in the first place. "How strange!" he thought to himself.

"We are persecuting the people in a land to which we came to free them from persecution. I don't understand why we are doing this and am ashamed to face the Yemenis because of this."

Masruq increased the dose of his persecution a little more with each passing day, killing whosoever he wanted and appropriating the wealth and property of anybody at will. When his cruelty reached insufferable proportions, Himyarite prince Sayf ibn Dhi Yazan rose against the occupying Abyssinians in their country. Getting wind of developments, Masruq ordered his commanders to quell the uprising in the harshest manner and teach the people a lesson they would never forget. The commanders obeyed and suppressed the revolt in a bloody way. They killed many young people. When Dhu Yazan saw that the people had no strength left to fight and resist, he betook himself to the presence of the Persian emperor, to seek his help to free Yemen from the Abyssinian yoke.

Giving Dhu Yazan audience, the emperor supposed Yemen to be far away and with limited sources of income. He, therefore, did not see the country as being fit for colonial interests. The Persian monarch did not provide Dhu Yazan with a definitive reply, stalling him off instead for a long time. He died in foreign lands waiting for the Sassanid emperor's reply.

His son Dhu Yazan's son Sayf was grieved at the news of his father's death and showed a great deal of effort to end the oppression. But he was not successful. The oppression, instead, intensified. Sayf could no longer endure his people being crushed more with each passing day and followed in his father's footsteps, going to Iran two years later. He received an audience with the emperor. With his sharp intelligence, he managed to persuade the emperor to provide help. He merged the eight thousand men coming from Iran with the militia he had gathered together and marched out against the Abyssinians. With the support of the people, victory was won within a short period of time. A large group of Abyssinians were killed during the war and some captured.[2]

Rabah, who had come to Yemen as a commander, was among the captives. When his hands were tied he felt his life fall apart and his thoughts and dreams for the future had faded away. His life had been turned upside down because of somebody's ambition for power and rued the day he came to Yemen.

---

[2]   Bayhaqi, *Dala'il an-Nubuwwa*, 1:297; Abu Nu'aym, *Dala'il an-Nubuwwa*, 51; Ibn al-Jawzi, *Muntazam*, 2:276; Kala'i, *Al-Iktifa*, 1:116; Diyarbakri, *Tarikh al-Khamis, 1:139.*

AT THE SLAVE MARKET

Rabah's hands were bound tight by the Yemenis in the lands to which he came as a soldier. He was pushed around for a long time and left without food or water. When things settled, he was taken to the slave market along with others, like him, who were taken captive. He couldn't believe what he was going through and as he pondered how dramatically his life had changed in such a short time, he felt as though he was going to go mad.

When being taken to the market, his heart, overcome with fear and apprehension, felt like it was going to stop. Endless questions plagued his mind. Throughout the journey he thought about this disaster that had befallen him and what would follow. What would happen now? To whom would he be sold? How would he live with his freedom ripped away from him? What would be the point of living if the free will that made one a human being was given to another? The questions were nonstop and tormented him until they reached the slave market.

The sounds surrounding Rabah at his arrival made his blood run cold. People bound in chains were being pushed and shoved and were being bought and sold like chattel. The whips drawing curves in the air were snapping on the backs of the poor souls sold as slaves and the blood flowing from their bodies trickled down from their feet.

The slaves kept in a barn-like place were being brought out in turns and offered for sale by criers. Rabah's angst only grew as those around him were sold off one by one. When it occurred to him that he had no other choice but to surrender to his Lord, he calmed down a little. While he battled with his emotions, his turn had come.

Somebody held the end of the rope with which his hands were bound and pulled him to the market site like an animal. The crier circled around him to ascertain his particular characteristics. He asked a few questions to learn of his circumstances. He then offered Rabah for sale, proclaiming words of praise. The Meccan slave trader Abdullah ibn Jud'an bought Rabah, impressed by what he saw. Rabah was deeply grieved at his predicament. He sought refuge in his Lord and set off on his journey in entreaty and reliance on Him. They continued on their way to the accompaniment of whips and the other purchased slaves. They reached Mecca after a long journey.

He was devastated from the first day he realized that those who bought the slaves did not view or treat them as human beings. His heart burned in pain and anguish. His spiritual suffering was too much to bear. All the more painful was the fact that there seemed to be nothing he could do to escape this persecution. All this was enough to cause him to abandon his hopes and dreams for the future, from just day one. A bitter event he was witness to at the time enabled him to see the painful predicament of those who had fallen prey to despair. He decided that no matter what he was to experience from that day forth, he would endure it patiently and hold on to life. Who knows, perhaps this desperation was the beginning of brand new hopes for him and others like him. The only thing he needed to do was to wait patiently.

Stripped of his freedom, Rabah told himself that he needed to cling on to the lifebuoy of patience in mind, that he needed to accept what had happened and hold on to life. He strove to this end, but this just didn't happen. He could not bring himself to accept being treated like an animal. His life had become a prison. For a long time, he lost the will to live and became unable to use his faculties of thought and feeling. This was also the direction the milieu in which he continued his existence forced him into as the system turned him and others like him into robots that heard and obeyed only the orders of their master.

A fixation on his master's orders meant that he had forgotten himself. He gave up on his dreams and lost sight of his future expectations, one by one. It took him a long time to get over his shock. Months went by. Once he got used to his predicament he got lost in his thoughts once again.

How terrifying it was being in a foreign land, living among people he didn't know, and with his fate in the hands of certain others. Just thinking about such a state was enough to send a person out of their wits. But life went on. Living in constant sorrow and suffering was just not feasible. He needed to accept his situation, cling to life, and free himself from the vortex of despair.

The more he thought, the more he shook off his despair. He began adapting to his situation, accepting all that befell him, and trying to hold on to whatever he could of life. So began his endeavor to establish a place for himself in society, even if with his slave identity. When the way he looked at events changed, his life changed with it.

HAMAMA

Hamama was the daughter of one of Abyssinia's noble families. She had set off towards Yemen either for travel, trade or some other intention, after Yemen's occupation by Abyssinian forces. The first thing she did upon arriving in Sana'a was to visit Qulays, Abraha's temple. She could not believe her eyes when she saw it. It was even more beautiful than had been described. She was awe-stricken at having beheld its interior.

Sana'a was a beautiful city and its people were warm and welcoming. She was happy that she had come and enjoyed being in Sana'a. Her happiness, however, did not last very long. Abraha's ambition unnerved her also. She was horrified at hearing of the destruction of the army that had come to demolish the Ka'ba, under a barrage of stones carried by birds. Worried for the Abyssinians and for herself, Hamama wanted to leave the land without a minute's delay and return, but this didn't happen. The situation did not allow for this.

She remained in Sana'a a while longer. Instead of learning from their father's mistakes, Abraha's sons followed suit when they succeeded him. Enslaved by their thirst for power, they, too, persecuted the people. Their oppression was enough to make Hamama ashamed of her Abyssinian identity.

No tyranny could continue forever. Their oppression also had an end. Sayf ibn Dhi Yazan, who had received help from the Persian emperor, faced the Abyssinians. He fought and defeated the oppressors, with most of the Abyssinians killed and survivors taken prisoner. Hamama rued not returning to her homeland and was taken captive during fighting. Her fear had seemingly caused her to lose consciousness. She was at a loss as to what to do and had forgotten everything but how to cry. Her freedom had been taken away and she was shortly thereafter taken to a slave market. She could not bring herself to accept the situation she had fallen into and kept her head lowered in shame.

That day, the day she was sold as chattel, was a day she would never ever forget. The voice of the criers rang in her ears for years. Sales began with an auction of slaves. Her heart rate increased as those next to her were sold off. When her turn came, she wanted to die there and then. Because even her crying was prohibited, she shed her tears inwardly. The voices of the men whose gaze struck great fear in her heart were like flies droning inside her head.

When auction began, there were many bidders. Whoever gave more money to the oppressors who put a price on her life was to possess her. When he took her home, he would treat her howsoever he wanted. He would get angry when he wanted, hurl insults at her when he wanted, and beat her purely because he felt like it. What a barbaric order was this, what a grotesque trade!

She was bought by slave trader Abdullah ibn Jud'an from the Banu Jumah. The Meccan merchant had bought a large number of slaves and concubines in addition to her. Just as he was about to return to Mecca, he ordered his men to tie the slaves to each other. They set off once preparations were complete. It was a long and arduous journey and they reached Mecca after having traversed vast deserts. Orders began flying without even a moment's rest.

Hamama was engrossed in her thoughts the whole way and faced the reality of her experience. The smartest thing she could do in this situation was to do what was asked of her to the best of her ability and avoid being tossed about from here to there until hope of freedom appeared. This was what she had decided. This is exactly what she did. She managed to stay put by doing all that was asked of her. Abdullah ibn Jud'an was pleased with her service and never thought of selling Hamama to another. As such, Hamama remained in Mecca where she would in later years live out the most beautiful days of her life.

LIVES THAT CONTINUED IN MECCA

Even if Hamama's facing the facts made her life easier, this was not always the case. She could not escape the long-standing depression she suffered as a result of her inability to stomach the persecution she faced from time to time. She lived as though she was not in her right mind. But nobody cared about what she went through, what she felt, and her psychological state. Her master fired orders at her constantly and demanded that they be completed perfectly. Whips cracked relentlessly against her back with the slightest flaw or omission.

Hamama knew how to learn from all that she witnessed. When she realized what she would face when she fell into despair, she would come to her senses and compose herself once more without being shoved about any further. To recover quickly throughout this time, she strove to maintain her will to survive by putting aside her fears, her fears and concerns, and her dreams for the future.

On one of these days, she met Rabah, an Abyssinian slave like herself. He, too, was a slave of Abdullah ibn Jud'an. He had been taken prisoner at Yemen also. All the things they had in common enabled their hearts to warm toward each other in a short time. After deciding that they were right for one another, they sought permission from their master and married. Before long, their mutual affection grew and their lives gained new meaning.

As one month followed the other in Mecca, Rabah received news one morning that would change his life. This was the best news he had received in a long time. This was one of the rare moments of happiness he had felt since his enslavement. His wife was pregnant and his eyes lit up when she gave him the glad tidings, but his happiness was not long-lived. Everything that rushed to his mind extinguished the light in his eyes. He responded to his wife with a bitter smile. The thought that his unborn child would come to the world as a slave just like himself cut short his happiness. This had put out the flicker in his eyes and erased the smile which flashed across his face.

How could he be happy! His child would not be able to enjoy their childhood, and run freely and play. Who would have delighted at having a child who would be born in darkness and drift towards the unknown? Which father would want this for their child? Who would want a child who would be shoved about by other kids, despised and held in contempt before his very eyes.

But he wanted a child all the same. Against all the odds, he wanted it with the hope that it would bring joy and comfort to their home. His hopes were not in vain. The child delighted his parents even before it was born. He removed the ashes heaped over the feelings they thought had all but disappeared and reignited their love, compassion and mercy.

Hamama gave birth alone, in a corner of the house, and shed tears of happiness for a long time to follow. Her husband shared her joy. They held their child in a warm embrace, caressing him and crying tears of joy.

In spite of everything, the black Abyssinian slave family had experienced happiness. To the child that was born in the sacred city of Mecca four years after what became known in Arab history as the Year of the Elephant and that was the subject of an entire Qur'anic chapter, Rabah and Hamama gave the name Bilal.[3]

Despite their sadness at knowing that their son would be a slave just like themselves, that he would be pushed around, and that he would never know the meaning of freedom or enjoy the honor of being human, they were still happy. Their lives changed after the birth of their son. While it got a little more difficult, it gained new meaning and beauty. Like the spring wherein strong winds blew, their days were pleasant, even if difficult.

The couple ultimately had three wonderful children: Bilal, Khalid and Ghufayra. They each became the joy of their home and heart. The children grew up in Mecca and shared the fate of their parents, becoming slaves just like them. They grew up without knowing what childhood was, without playing and laughing with friends, without breathing the air of freedom, and without having anything which they could call their own. They merely worked. This is what they did for a lifetime.

BILAL AL-HABASHI

Bilal al-Habashi was born as a slave, living without a sense of servitude until the age of four or five. He ran and played to his heart's content, without interference by others. A few years later, he had a brother by the name of Khalid and a sister named Ghurayfa. The family was further animated with their arrival. While their living conditions were difficult, they grew up blissfully unaware and happily.

When Bilal reached seven or eight, he began to experience a sense of enslavement and began working at a very young age. Along with his friends, slaves like himself, he drove herds of sheep to the mountains of Mecca. There, he tended to the animals of Abdullah ibn Jud'an throughout the whole day. For as long as he could remember, Bilal worked as a shepherd, without a care for the scorching heat of the sun or the rugged mountain ranges. What else could he do besides?

By the time he reached early adulthood, he was a tall, thin youth of rather dark complexion. His days as a slave passed working at an intense pace. Being half-hungry meant that he was very skinny. Thick, grayish hair crowned his head.

---

[3] Ibn Sa'd, *Tabaqat*, 7:385.

Up until his mid-thirties, he worked herding sheep, serving his master, and striving to please his steward.[4]

His master Abdullah ibn Jud'an worked the able-bodied, very intelligent and resourceful Bilal for years on end without making even the smallest effort to get to know him. This was because he did not recognize his slaves unless there was a major problem or extenuating circumstance, knowing only their numbers. Just as he was not concerned with their social lives and their abilities, he paid not the slightest attention to their feelings, needs or problems. More often than not, he would even ignore the fact that they were human, would be rude and rough with them when he saw them, thinking only of how he could exploit their physical strength. Except in special cases, he did not think about identifying their particular abilities and benefiting from them. Such an injudicious attitude meant that slaves were no different to a camel or a sheep in the eyes of their master. They made do with taking advantage of their physical strength.

JOURNEY TO DAMASCUS

The remarkably clever and resourceful Bilal al-Habashi, was recognized immediately by Abdullah ibn Jud'an's steward. Knowing Bilal since his childhood, the steward would call for him whenever there was an important task to be undertaken. On one such occasion, the Meccans were busy with preparations for a trade caravan to go to Damascus. Abdullah ibn Jud'an summoned his steward, directing him to join the caravan. The steward readied the goods to be sold and handed them over to the head of the caravan.

Just as preparations neared completion, the steward sought trusted individuals whom he could send with the caravan to protect Abdullah ibn Jud'an's goods. After giving it long thought a few names stood out. Bilal al-Habashi was one of them. It grieved Bilal that he would be separated from his family when he heard that he was going to Damascus. But he was no doubt also excited at the prospect of seeing different lands.

The caravan set off after all preparations were complete. The road was long and the journey hard. They had to cross several deserts to get to Damascus. Somebody in particular caught his attention during the journey. That he was a good person was clear in his every manner. He tried to be near him and

---

4   Baladhuri, *Ansab al-Ashraf*, 1:207–208; Ibn Manzur, *Mukhtasar*, 5:203.

speak to him throughout the journey. This man was the young merchant well known to the Meccans, Abu Bakr.

Bilal al-Habashi's beautiful voice made his task a lot easier. Listening to his poetry recitals while traveling through the desert, Abu Bakr would say, "What a beautiful voice you have. It has relieved our travel weariness and has brought the distant near."

The poems he read were instrumental in the attention he received and the guidance he was shown in way of getting things done easily. When they reached the city of Busra, south of Damascus, they set up camp. Tents were pitched and a night's rest was followed by a visit to the market. They lined up their goods for sale. If they sold all their goods, they would buy new ones and return to Mecca. Otherwise, they would continue on to Damascus.

Abu Bakr saw a dream during the journey and awoke in horror. The dream he saw was not one that was of the common kind. He could not shake it off for quite time. He was anxious all the way until Busra. The first thing he did when he got to city was to go to a priest to have his dream interpreted. The most famous priest in the region was Bahira. The first person Abu Bakr asked directed him to Bahira. Abu Bakr took Bilal with him. They went straight to Bahira when they reached the church. As soon as the priest saw them, he asked,

"Yes! What can I do for you?" "I wish to speak with the priest,"

Abu Bakr replied. "I'm the priest,"

Bahira said, "Who might you be?"

"I am Abu Bakr ibn Abi Quhafa," he said.

"Where are you from?" Bahira continued.

"I am from Mecca," Abu Bakr answered. The questions continued.

"What is your tribe?"

"I am of the Quraysh."

"What has brought you here?"

"We're here on business." When Bahira inquired, "For what do you visit me?" Abu Bakr related to him his dream and requested that he interpret it.

Bahira said, "You have seen a beautiful dream indeed. May Allah make your dream come true!" He then interpreted Abu Bakr's dream saying, "One from among your people will be sent as a Prophet. You will believe in him. You will be his vizier during his life and his caliph after his demise."

Abu Bakr was astonished by what he heard and was taken for words. He requested that the Christian priest give information about the Prophet he spoke of. Bahira could not turn him down and described the last Prophet that would be sent to humanity: "This person sent by Allah as the last Messenger will invite people to belief in the One Allah, denouncing the worship of idols."

Stunned, Abu Bakr and his companion Bilal knew the Arabs would never allow such a thing, exclaiming,

"Really? Will he be able to do so despite the Quraysh?"

"Indeed!" Bahira responded. "Allah will protect him from the Quraysh and from the Arabs."

The two listened carefully to Bahira's words and when he finished, they asked for his leave and returned to the caravan.[5]

A BLACK SLAVE IN MECCA

Bilal al-Habashi had been greatly affected by what he had experienced in Busra with Abu Bakr. On the way back, he thought constantly of Bahira's words. His life as a black slave continued from where he left off on his return to Mecca. When the things he experienced and witnessed as a slave seared his heart, when his feelings were hurt and his pride wounded, when his selfhood was filed away and faded a little more with each passing day, and when he was made to forget his humanity more and more, he forever remembered that day. He would recall everything he heard from Bahira while in Busra and keep his hope for the future alive.

Like every other slave, his life was as difficult as to defy description. His life and everything pertaining to it depended on the words that would come out of his master's mouth. He could not think on his own behalf, ask for anything, or want anything, and even if he wanted anything, he could not do anything to obtain it. He could not have any thoughts or even dreams for the future.

Slavery destroys a person's faculty of thought, their ability to put their thoughts into practice, to generate ideas and to reason, and takes away their willpower. It gives them no right to speak, even ignoring that they carry the characteristics that make them human. Slaves had no value whatsoever in the eyes of their master. No matter how hard they worked, no matter what they accomplished, they still were at best half fed and half hungry.

---

5   Ibn Manzur, *Mukhtasar*, 13:39; Sahhar, *Bilal Mu'adhdhin ar-Rasul*, 8.

Slavery takes away people's freedom and even their lives. It forever crushes and destroys them before their hopes even have the chance of flourishing. It stifles any zest for life. It destroys their hopes for the future and turns them into individuals trying to hold on to life and struggling merely to survive. This was precisely the kind of life Bilal led and except for a few incidents, such as the one involving Bahira, he seemed to have no hope for the future. The only things connecting him to life were such words and experiences.

"Who knows? Maybe I will live to witness these days?" he thought to himself in hopeful anticipation. "Maybe I can even throw off this yoke of slavery." He, like others, did not know who the awaited Prophet was. But he was acquainted with such exemplary personalities as Muhammad ibn Abdullah and Abu Bakr ibn Abi Quhafa who made no distinction between slave and those who were free, valuing only the human being. As he saw them and heard of their laudable behavior, he was reminded of his own humanity. While the Meccans did not even view slaves as human, far from holding them in contempt, they would converse with them and—as in the case of the Ammar ibn Yasir—did not hesitate to make friends with them.

Crushed under the weight of slavery, Bilal felt comfortable only in the presence of a few, like the Messenger of Allah, and in nature. When he took to the mountains and wilderness to tend livestock, he forgot his enslavement, even if for a short time. Nature's inspiriting air seemed to breathe peace into his soul. While chasing the sheep on the mountain foothills, he found himself. His soul broke free of the shackles of slavery one by one and flapped its wings towards freedom.

Who was to say, perhaps there was still hope.

While there was still life there was still hope, and there could be no despair in Allah.

As he lived, Bilal was to come to better learn this truth.

A SPIRIT THAT BREAKS FREE

Enslavement became more insufferable as one got older. Taking to the mountains and herding sheep was no longer enough to make Bilal forget his enslavement, as was the case during his younger years. Such a sense crushed him a little more each day. At times, the world in all its expanse became so constricted for him, and his soul felt as though it would come out of his body and leave him. He was looking for a single light. One that, even if faint, would light up his path and give him hope.

Alas! Heaven forbid one be seen to be weak! How could one find light where even the free were oppressed, their property and lives usurped, and their honor readily encroached upon?

Wherever he looked, wheresoever he turned, he saw nothing save the dense darkness of ignorance. He lived in a world where moral decay, corruption, selfishness, and desire took precedence over everything else. He felt like he was drowning. He wanted to exclaim with all his strength, to take a stance against ignorance, egotism, and corruption. He wanted to confront those who took his freedom away and cry out to the throngs: "Stop! This road is a dead-end!"

This was the point where the darkness was darkest. There was not a glimmer of hope, a sign of light anywhere. Who knows, maybe there was, but he couldn't see it. He resisted all he could not to lose all hope and looked again and again about him for any sight of a light.

His patience quest would finally lead him to a light. There was a luminous light very near which would illuminate the entire world. A light that would be a beacon of hope for all humanity and that would protect the downtrodden, the ill-treated, those whose rights were so easily taken away from them, the weak and the powerless.

A light that would put a stop to the oppressors and that would embrace not only the free, but slaves as well. A light that would abolish the distinction between rich and poor, powerful and weak, ruler and the ruled being an instrument for oppression and persecution, prevent its being an obstacle to fellowship and solidarity, and embrace all of society's segments without labeling them this or that.

A light that would bandage wounds with mercy and compassion, uphold right, truth and justice, bring love and respect to the fore, see differences in race, religion and language not as a means for separation but as enrichment, and that promised not only worldly peace, but peace in the eternal realm also.

While Bilal spent his time away from the city, tending sheep and camels on the mountains, some of his friends made trips to the city and back on various occasions. What they related to him on their return broke up the dark clouds that enveloped his heart, illuminated his path, and nourished the seeds of hope that he had hidden in the innermost part of his heart since the day he saw Bahira. He thought about going to the city as soon as possible to meet that fine person who reminded him of his humanity, declared that all human beings, free and slave, were as equal as the teeth on a comb, and that nobody had the right to make any other servant or slave. He wanted to listen to him, find peace in his company, relieve the pain he felt in his heart, and taste the feeling of freedom. But how could he do this? He was a slave. He was at the beck and call of his master. What is more, his master had declared war on that light that had risen on Mecca's horizon.

Hard times were waiting for Bilal al-Habashi and those like him.

Eventually, Bilal found a way of escaping to the city without regard for what would befall him. Thus began his secret search for Muhammad ibn Abdullah, whom he had admired and whose manner and conduct he thought highly of even before his Prophethood. He trusted that when he found him, the hopes that had begun to fade would be revived anew. He needed this more than he needed food and water, even more than he needed air. But this did not happen. While he looked for him all over, he could not find him. Once again, with a heart filled with sorrow, he left the city and returned to his mountain where he was able to breathe comfortably—to his silence.

No doubt, had he known what he would experience some time later, his sorrow would have been replaced by joy. Allah would reunite him with His Messenger, away from the city's atmosphere of disquiet and concern, in an environment where he could speak comfortably.

What Bilal was going to witness at this reunion was way beyond any of his expectations. For this Messenger was going to promise not just freedom from the shackles of slavery that other human beings had fastened around his ankles, but also freedom from the whims and desires that the carnal self and Satan had clamped across the door of his heart. He would call to happiness in this world and the Hereafter, offering the water of life necessary for the regrowth and revival of the tree of life on the verge of desiccation.

Wadin ibn Ata describes Bilal's first encounter with Allah's Messenger, peace and blessings be upon him, and his acceptance of Islam in the following way:

Some time after the beginning of Divine revelation, the period of inviting people to Islam had begun. Meccan leaders who had become aware of the Messenger's words had become excessively disturbed by this. They exerted a great deal of pressure on the people to keep them away from him. It came to the point where no one dared exchange words with Allah's Messenger. There would be great tension if anyone did do so, and the tension only escalated. To prevent this from happening, the Messenger of Allah would leave Mecca with his close friend Abu Bakr, retreating to a cave outside the city, and preferred to stay out of sight for a while.

One day, they had again withdrawn from Mecca to seek sanctuary in a cave. While worshiping their Lord on the one hand, they made an assessment of the situation on the other and wait for things to settle.

As they were here, Abdullah ibn Jud'an's slave Bilal al-Habashi was grazing his master's flock of sheep, as was customary. Oblivious to the great miracle waiting for him and that would completely change his life, he eventually came all the way to the cave in which Allah's Messenger and Abu Bakr were waiting. All the while, his mind was preoccupied with thoughts of Muhammad, upon him be peace and blessings, who was so talked about in Mecca.

Who was he?

What was he like?

What exactly was he saying?

To what was he inviting the people in secret?

The questions plaguing his mind were endless. He tended the sheep unaware that he passed in front of the cave the person he sought was in and that he would meet him a matter of minutes.

Seeing Bilal al-Habashi, the Messenger of Allah was delighted he had the opportunity of inviting yet another person to Islam. By way of sparking conversation, he called out, "O shepherd, do have some milk that you can give us?"

When Bilal looked up he saw two people in their middle ages. Their faces were glowing and they were unlike all the people that he had seen thus far. They were smiling at the slave that others did not even look at, and were treating him as a normal human being. He felt some warmth in his heart at first sight of them.

Could one of them have been the person who had been inviting people to belief in secret?

If so, what should he have done? How should he have behaved?

The questions chased one another in his mind. Bilal collected himself with the Messenger's repeating his question. Bilal got through the day with just a bowl of milk, and were he to give that away, he would go hungry. Thus, he said grudgingly, "No, I do not have any milk that I can give you. Only one of the sheep gives milk and this one I milk for my food. I have nothing else for food."

"Would you sell it to me?" the Messenger of Allah asked.

Bilal did not know what to say. The person he had wanted to see for such a long time, and the desire of seeing whom he had been so afraid to voice, even to his own self, perchance stood before him. What is more, there was no one else around to see them. He could easily listen to him here and learn about what he called the people to.

Even if his fears caused slight hesitation, his heart brimmed with the happiness and peace at having found what it was looking for. He quickly herded his sheep and went to him. Sensing Bilal's emotion and hesitation, the Messenger of Allah took a step towards him by way of removing the barriers on the path to guidance.

"Could you give me a cup?" he requested.

Bilal had his eyes fixed of Allah's Messenger, watching in awe and astonishment at the esteem he was afforded. He no longer cared at remaining hungry.

"Of course," he said. He retrieved the cup with great joy and handed it over to the Messenger of Allah for him to milk the sheep. Allah's Messenger headed straight to the animal and milked it until the container was filled. He then drank from it first and then passed it to Abu Bakr who was right beside him. Abu Bakr, too, drank to his fill and there was still milk left in the cup. The Messenger handed the remaining milk to Bilal. Bilal, too, drank to satiation and then sought permission to sit with them afterwards. The Messenger of Allah, who saw him not as a slave but as a human being, indicated for him to sit saying, "Have a seat." Bilal was being treated not like a slave, but as though he were one of the nobles of Mecca. After the Messenger of Allah inquired after Bilal, their discussion began. During the conversation, the Prophet told Bilal that he was indeed the Messenger sent by Allah. He read from the Qur'an and told him about Islam. Every word Bilal heard reverberated in his heart and he was utterly stupefied. These could never have been the words of a mortal. It was clear that before him stood a Prophet. Such a thought only raised Bilal's excitement.

Bilal was listening to Allah's Messenger in absolute awe, and Allah's Messenger invited him to Islam. Bilal was stunned. He wanted with all his heart to recite the Declaration of Faith and embrace Islam, but remembering his master caused him to take a step back.

It was the very first time a freeman addressed himself to him as an ordinary human being, spoke to him courteously and without condescension. He was baffled, and as happy as he was baffled at the Messenger's approach to him. His succinct speech, the nobility in his manner of being and behavior, the beauty and sweetness in his words drew Bilal to him and won his heart over again and again.

In point of fact, it was enough that Bilal that he be treated as a human being and valued as such for his acceptance of Islam. The truthfulness of his words was not even necessary. But everything he said was truth and was as beautiful and noteworthy as it was beautiful.

He raised his head once again and looked at the Messenger of Allah. At that moment he felt a Divine light fill his heart. No hesitation remained. In complete earnestness he recited the Declaration of Faith and became a Muslim.

For a long time now, the Messenger of Allah had been subjected to the oppression and persecution of the Meccans, and he did not want Bilal or any of his other Companions to encounter any difficulty or be beaten and battered by the polytheists. For this reason he urged Bilal not to tell anyone that he had embraced Islam.

Bilal accepted and sought the Messenger's leave in great jubilation and enthusiasm. He gathered his flock and returned to his master's home. That day, the sheep had fed as much as to attract notice. This did not escape the attention of master either. Astonished at the phenomenal situation, his master addressed Bilal for the first time in years as a result. He summoned him.

"It seems that you've found a fine pasture for the sheep." Not wanting to raise any unnecessary suspicion, Bilal brushed over the matter saying, "Yes, I have found very fertile pasture."

In uttering these words, he thought about what a great grace and blessing he had attained by becoming acquainted with the Messenger of Allah.

He wanted so much to learn and carry out Islam's injunctions and wanted for it to take root in the innermost depths of his being. He knew that he needed to learn more about Islam for this to happen. He wanted to go to the Messenger of Allah, as soon as he possibly could, to learn the newly-revealed Qur'anic verses and looked forward to the next morning every night he came home. Each morning, he took his sheep straight to the cave where the Messenger of Allah retired, listened to him until the end of the day, and took in his knowledge and spiritual effusion. When it began to get dark he very reluctantly left the cave and headed home. His feet rebelled, as it were, and did not want to go home. But he had to go. For, he was still a slave. His will was not his own. With heavy heart he remembered this, bow his head, and silently head for his master's home.

He now impatiently waited for morning. As soon as the sun rose, he ran to the barn, took the sheep and went straight to the cave. Thus did he savor the honor and happiness of being able to listen to the Master of the Universe and spend time in his intimate company.[6]

THE POLYTHEISTS' SUSPICION

The enemy never sleeps and the Meccan polytheists would not sleep either. This sudden change in Bilal was noticed by his enemies as well as his careful friends. They wondered what was going on. But nobody except one dwelt much on it. This person was someone who became more vigilant after Allah's Messenger began inviting the Meccans to Islam, and observed his surroundings very closely and carefully. Nothing happening in Mecca escaped his notice. He would pick up on the smallest detail and investigate it further. This person was none other than the possessor of the epithet 'father of ignorance,' Abu Jahl, who instantly became informed of events. Abu Jahl was enemy of truth and devotee of ignorance.

As he once passed by Abdullah ibn Jud'an's house, he noticed the change in the sheep that were passing before him. Nothing went unnoticed, this detail included. He went straight to Abdullah ibn Jud'an.

"As far as I can see, your sheep have been well fed and are not in want of milk," he said. "What is the reason for this?" Abdullah replied,

---

6   Ibn Manzur, *Mukhtasar*, 5:203.

"You're right! The sheep have been feeding very well for the past three days and their milk has increased. I noticed this also, but couldn't understand how this happened."

The sharp-witted Abu Jahl believed that this was no ordinary incident and stemmed from an extraordinary circumstance. He thought for a while and tried to identify what this circumstance might be. Then he remembered the Messenger's being out of town for several days. It did not take long for him to put two and two together. Abu Jahl knew his enemy very well, even knowing that he was a Prophet, and supposed him to have something to do with this extraordinary situation. No! This was not a suspicion but the very truth itself. He turned to Abdullah ibn Jud'an and said, "I swear by the Lord of the Ka'ba, this slave of yours definitely knows where Abu Qabsha is. Don't let him go to the same place again or, Allah forbid, he will renounce his religion."

As this conversation took place, Allah's Messenger left the cave he had withdrawn to for a few days and returned to Mecca. In this way, even if Bilal was followed, his acceptance of Islam was not understood.

The Messenger's comments on slaves, that they were human beings like their masters and deserved to be valued as such, enraged slave owners and Meccan nobles. It unsettled them that since he had begun to convey the message of Islam and invite the people in secret, several slaves listening to him had embraced Islam. Meccan leaders viewed this as a dangerous development. The last thing they wanted was to lose their slaves and, on top of that, to see them as a counter force. They were worried that by affecting one another, the slaves would together become Muslim within a short period of time, and that their fears would become a reality. This is why they decided to take all slaves out of Mecca. Abdullah ibn Jud'an, who had the most slaves in the city, wasted no time and immediately summoned his steward. He ordered that all his slaves be removed from the city. The steward carried out these orders and took all the slaves, except Bilal and a few others, outside of Mecca.

Assuming that somebody who spent his entire day tending sheep on the mountain slopes outside the city could not have been informed of events, the steward felt no need to send Bilal and a handful of others along with the other slaves. He was very happy with their service and character. Bilal's situation was instrumental in his superior's decision. Not being around during the day and returning to the city only after everyone had retired to their homes helped. One of the reasons for keeping him in the city was for there to be somebody to see to his needs when he got back.[7]

From the day he entered the folds of Islam Bilal's soul attained great peace and though physically he was a slave, he was free intellectually and spiritually. He no longer unmindfully worshiped Lat and Uzza, nor was he a slave to his masters. The light of belief has shone upon his mind as well as his heart. No longer would anybody be able to rule his heart, nor induce him to worship idols made of wood or stone which could avail him not. They could not estimate his masters too highly and present them as semi-gods in his eyes. His heart belonged to Allah alone. Bilal believed in Him wholeheartedly and worshiped Him in utmost sincerity.

His masters could have only ruled over his physical being. With this belief and resolve, he shut tight the doors of his heart to the oppressors, and opened them wide to Allah, His Messenger, and those loved by them. He admitted only them in the palace of his heart and deemed inclination to them, abasement. He turned away from the mentality enslaving human beings and from its deities, putting the greatest distance between himself and them. He would never bow down before an idol, even if his master commanded him to do so, and would not be unmindful. For, he was now able to think like a free person, could evaluate events, and understand the truth for what it was. He was no longer a wretched slave who was unaware even of the existence of his own volition, whose mind and soul was stolen. He would never be again.

There was not only the life of this world for him. There was a life more important than the worldly one. The Messenger of Allah had explained to him that there would be a life beyond this worldly life, one which was eternal. To attain bounties in Paradise that eyes could not see, ears could not hear, and minds could not conceive of, every individual, free or slave, needed to keep away from evils that would endanger their happiness in the Hereafter for the sake of the fleeting pleasures of the world. How could he have turned a blind eye to truths that were so manifest? What else could consciously reverting to the worship of idols, knowing that they consisted of nothing but rock, or a piece of wood, have been but foolishness?

---

[7] Ibn Manzur, *Mukhtasar*, 5:203.

From now on, he would not turn away from Islam even if his master killed him for it, and he would never give up the freedom of his spirit, heart and very core, and was not turning away from the idols and fulfilling the injunctions of Islam a necessity of being human? Could it at all have been possible for him to go back once he had been freed of being a mere piece of property and seeing that he was *ashraf al-makhluqat*, the noblest of all creation? He accomplished this too. Even if his body was enslaved, he had emancipated his heart and soul and had reunited his them with everlasting freedom.

FAMILY EMBRACES ISLAM

Bilal's inner world became luminous after entering the fold of Islam, and those feelings that had for years laid lifeless came back to life. He wanted to share these wonderful feelings with his family right away and for them to attain spiritual freedom also. At the very first opportunity, he went to his mother Hamama and his siblings Khalid and Ghufayra. He explained with great enthusiasm the extraordinary moments he experienced with Allah's Messenger and related all that he heard from him. He spoke about how wrong it was to worship idols, and that deliverance and happiness in the world and the Hereafter was possible only through belief in Allah and His Messenger. Bilal's audience listened carefully to every word that came out of his mouth and were very impressed with what they heard. But they were as scared and nervous.

"Please don't speak of such things so openly elsewhere," they warned. "If our masters get wind of this they'll kill us." Bilal was well aware of the danger and he assured them that he had spoken to nobody other than them. He then invited them to Islam saying, "Please give up your worship of idols and believe in Allah and His Messenger."

Hamama, who had until this day hidden her Christian belief even from her own children out of fear, was deeply moved by what her son told her. She went back to her childhood and youth and remembered what the priests used to say about idols and the last Prophet to be sent to humankind. How similar these words were to what her son was now saying! It was clear that the person who said that he was a Messenger was the awaited last Prophet the priests foretold. She wanted to recite the Declaration of Faith without delay and profess her belief in Islam. But she could not. She thought of what would befall her if she did. She did not even want to think about what the polytheists would do to her when they found out, what cruelties they would subject her to. She said, addressing her son: "I believe in every word that you say. But allow us some time to think." Bilal was pleased with such a response.

"Yes," he said, "take as much time as you need." It did not take long. Plucking up her courage, Hamama embraced Islam along with her daughter.[8]

The lives of his newly-Muslim mother and sister gained meaning just like his had done. Their way of living changed for the better and their home was filled with joy. From that day forth, they too began to see themselves as a human being like everyone else, to look with hope at their lives to come, and to dream of a good future. Islam, for them, became a great beacon of hope.

DIVINE LOVE OVERFLOWING FROM THE HEART

Bilal al-Habashi was very careful in the matter of hide his acceptance of Islam, as Allah's Messenger had advised him to do, and took utmost caution to ensure that this was not understood. He refrained from doing anything that might arise their suspicions. He did not tell anybody except his family that he had become a Muslim, not even his closest associates. He could not conceal it all the same. He had been destined for trial in this regard.

After having embraced Islam, Bilal grew in love for the Ka'ba. He would visit it whenever he found the opportunity and circumambulate it again and again. Afterwards, he would sit beside one of its corners, engage in contemplation, illuminate his inner world and thus attain repose. On precisely one of these days, he left home early in the morning and went to the Ka'ba at a time when he thought nobody else would be there. He looked around and was relieved to have seen no one there. He looked again and again to make sure. He could not see anybody. After circumambulation, he sat by the Ka'ba and delved into his thoughts. A group of members of the Quraysh who had come in the meantime had seated themselves near the Ka'ba and were deep in conversation. As they were speaking quietly, Bilal had not noticed them. Bilal was overcome by an intensity of feeling during his reflection and was unable to contain him-

---

[8]   Ibn Hajar, *Isaba*, 11555; Ibn Manzur, *Mukhtasar*, 7:331.

self. He stood up. He looked long and hard at the idols—the symbol of the mindset that had stripped him of his freedom and persecuted him for years on end, the symbol of oppression and slavery.

He did not avert his gaze for even a second. It was as though he wanted to avenge the anger and rage that had built inside him over all these years. He looked around again, and still could not see anybody. Overcome as he was with the emotional intensity he was experiencing which enveloped his heart and engulfed his inner world, Bilal had failed to notice the Meccans sitting on the other side of the Ka'ba. He released all this anger by spitting in the face of the idol that was positioned right next to him and shouting out the things that his heart could no longer contain. He spat on the idol on the one hand while screaming with all his might on the other.

"Debased be those who worship you! Debased be those who worship you!"

The people of the Quraysh who heard him jumped from their seats in their effort to see what was going on. They ran in the direction of the voice. They had heard everything so clearly and were bristling with rage. Bilal who had been so at ease on the assumption that nobody else was there, was taken aback when he saw the men standing before him.

"What did you just say?" they boomed. "Did you just curse our gods and us who worship them?"

At that moment, it was as if all of Bilal's fears had disappeared and an immense courage overtook his heart. He didn't hold back.

"Yes!" he exclaimed. "I cursed them."

The hero who was proclaiming the truth with Divine love knew for sure that the Meccan polytheists would sweep down on him from the moment he uttered this response. In a slave's reflex, he fled as soon as he finished his words. He ran and the Meccan polytheists chased him. He ran into the side streets to throw them off the track. They were hot on his trail until he reached Abdullah ibn Jud'an's residence, where he finally lost them. Bilal rushed into his master's house and hid.

The pursuers were certain that he was hiding inside. They stood at the entrance and began shouting at the top of their voice. Unaware of what had happened, Abdullah ibn Jud'an was baffled by the screaming in front of his house. He went out to find out what was going on. His confusion only increased when he saw the large crown standing outside.

"What is it?" he asked the men. "Why have you gathered here? Why are you shouting?" In a fit of rage, the men retorted, "Have you become an infidel?"

This was a most unexpected reaction as far as Abdullah ibn Jud'an was concerned and he was completely dumbfounded. As he looked at the men, he was trying to learn what had happened.

"Can you hear yourself?" he shot back. "How can you ascribe such things to someone like me? If you can prove that I have done such a thing, I will sacrifice a hundred camels in the name of Lat and Uzza."

"You say that, but your black slave just did such and such," they responded. "Then he ran away and hid in your house. Could he have done such a thing if he hadn't taken encouragement from you?"

Unable to get his head around what was happening, Abdullah called for his steward.

"What is the meaning of this?" he clamored. "Didn't I tell you to take all the slaves out of the city! What is that slave doing here? Find him and bring him here immediately."

The steward and his men set to finding Bilal. After a long search, they drew him out of his hiding place and dragged him off striking at him repeatedly. When they brought him to their master, he was covered in blood. Abdullah then realized the truth of what the people of the Quraysh were saying. He was all the more enraged at his steward. He began yelling at him once more.

"What's this? Hadn't I told you to send all the slaves away from Mecca?"

The steward bowed his head in shame and said, "Sir, he was tending the sheep outside the city coming home only in the evenings."

Abdullah was unwilling to continue the discussion further. He was more interested in averting the wrath of the Meccans at his doorstep. Indicating Bilal al-Habashi, he said, "Is this the man you're looking for? If so, I present him to you. Take him and do want you want." After handing his slave over, he left them angrily and went back inside.

Among the group were such Meccan leaders as Abu Jahl and Umayya ibn Khalaf. Umayya stepped forward and took the torture of Bilal personally upon himself. He grabbed him by the arm and handed him to his henchmen. The men bound Bilal tight. From there, they went to the courtyard of the Ka'ba. Umayya was ruthless and he did not just want to punish the slave who sniped at their idols by slapping him a few times. He had different intentions. He wanted to torture Bilal in such a way as would be spoken of far and wide and suppress any potential others. He thought it best to wait for the sun to be at its zenith for the torture to take full force and cause even greater agony. As it was still too early, he order them saying, "Take him home at once!"

While his men hurled Bilal away, he went to the notables of the Quraysh who had only just begun gathering. He related to them all that had happened and consulted them on the best course of action. They decided on taking Bilal out to the desert and torturing him.[9]

Bilal's mere physical enslavement was not enough for the Meccans. They wanted for every moment of his life to be tainted with pain and suffering. They wanted to enslave his heart and spirit and to control his mind. Like them, he too had to believe in the religion of their forebears and worship idols. If he didn't do this willingly, they were resolved to force him. If necessary, they would exact kinds of torture that nobody could have even imagined. This was because their experiences told them that the bodies of those people whose hearts and spirits they failed to enslave would one day assuredly escape captivity.

If Bilal al-Habashi was not a slave, Zayd ibn Harith was not a slave, Ammar ibn Yasir, then who would be?

Who would do their work? Who would serve them?

Whose master would they be, by crushing whom would they receive satisfaction, and who would they oppress?

How would the system of slavery they had established continue?

No, they would never let this happen. They could never allow Islam, nor any another religion, to do away with the slavery order they had so laboriously established. Nobody could liberate the people they had enslaved, by turning them into conscious individuals, and thus cast a shadow upon their mastership. To this end, they would show no mercy to anybody and would ruthlessly stamp out any who opposed their establishment. Anybody would be punished—whether spouse, friend or relative—in the severest possible way and killed if necessary. This is exactly what they did. They declared war on Islam and the Muslims. Thus began

[9]   Ibn Manzur, *Mukhtasar*, 5:204.

a struggle that would continue until the end of time. This was to be the incessant struggle between truth and falsehood, belief and unbelief.

THE TORTURE BEGINS

People whose heart and spirit have become free may work as slaves temporarily, but they can never be kept as such for good. Whatever the time and place, they will one day definitely spur into action and light the torch beginning their struggle for freedom. Consciously, fearlessly and unflinchingly, they struggle until the end with great wisdom. In this way, they break not just their own shackles, but the shackles of thousands who have been bound in chains just like them and free them from enslavement. Such tyrants as Abu Jahl and Umayya knew this very well and so they would give no respite whatsoever to those people whose hearts and spirits broke free.

The Meccan leaders who knew all too well that Islam accepts every human being as the most honorable of creation—without differentiating between wealthy or poor, powerful or weak—holds that superiority is not by virtue of wealth or possessions, position or rank, and vehemently rejects servitude to another human being, declared war on it for precisely this reason. It was not difficult for Abdullah in Jud'an and those like him to predict that those slaves who became acquainted with Islam would struggle for their freedom, and so they removed them from the city to prevent their contact with the Muslims.

When they learned of Bilal's conversion, therefore, despite all their sensitivity on the subject and all the precautionary measures they had taken, they were most alarmed.

How did this slave become a Muslim?

Where have we gone wrong?

Why have we failed despite all the pressure we have exerted?

What if other slaves followed suit? These were some of the questions preying at their minds. It would be too late if they did not take urgent measures. When the torch of liberty had been lit, it could never again be extinguished. The Meccan leaders were aware of the gravity of the matter. They dropped everything to pursue Bilal al-Habashi, who in fact had not even the worth of a gnat in their eyes. They followed him all the way to his master's house. They took him with force.

The next step was obvious: making him rue the day he embraced Islam by tormenting him beyond endurance. Added to this was striking fear in the hearts of other slaves through Bilal's person, and ensuring they avoid even being seen side-by-side with a Muslim.

As soon as Umayya ibn Khalaf deliberated with the Meccan nobles and got their approval to torture Bilal, he had Bilal taken from the house when the sun began to rise, knowing that he himself would be under the scorching sun too. The thugs who had tightly bound the Prophet's Companion took him out. When Umayya approached them, he instructed, "Drag him through the streets so he can be an example to all others."

The men complied, making a quick pull at the rope to bring Bilal to the ground, and kicking him when he tried to get up. They dragged him across the streets of Mecca. The Companion's cries fell on deaf ears, and the brutes turned a blind eye to his being covered in blood.

There were mixed reactions from the people who spilled out on to the streets as they passed by. Some laughed and made merry, others took pity, while others still, said such things as, "Serves you right! This is the punishment for turning against our idols!"

Bilal, however, was barely conscious. He was not in a position to see the eyes fixed on, nor the words directed at him. He was taken to the desert writhing in intense pain.

The men were exhausted from taking him through one street after the other. They left Bilal, on the verge of passing out, on the fiery sands and sat down to rest, jumping back up a few minutes later on the orders of Umayya ibn Khalaf. They placed the Prophet's Companion on the burning sands and tied his hands and feet to stakes nailed into the ground. Umayya breathed fire as he walked up to him and pressed down on Bilal's shoulders with his dirty feet.

"Deny Muhammad!" he screamed. Failing to get a response, he pressed again will even more force.

"Deny Muhammad! Deny Muhammad!"

Unable to get the answer he wanted to hear, Umayya was foaming at the mouth and kicked Bilal, threatening him.

"Deny Muhammad, or face a dire end!"

There was still no answer from Bilal. Umayya did not know what to do. "What obstinacy is this!" he thought to himself. "I will be a laughing stock." Umayya's ruthless hand was uncontrollable. He flew into a rage, took hold of the whip and stormed towards Bilal. He whipped him until he blacked out. Exasperated, he turned to his men, shouting, "Bring him round immediately and continue the torture." The men poured the bucket of water they had brought with them all over Bilal and kicked him until he regained consciousness. Umayya stood beside Bilal once more.

"Come to your senses! We're going to keep at it until you deny Muhammad!" Still no response... The hero of Islam who was ready to take on every kind of difficulty and torment for the sake of his belief responded only with a bitter smile.

When the enemies of Islam failed to get what they want, they brought him round again and again. They tortured him to the point of exhaustion and be him almost to death. But no matter what they did, not a single word but truth fell from Bilal's lips.[10]

Bilal's only crime was his belief in the existence and unity of Allah and his striving to be a good person. He could not for the life of him understand why the Meccan polytheists were so afraid of him and others like him and just could not make sense of the reason for their anger.

No matter how angry the Meccans became, the extent of the cruelties they inflicted on him, they could not have caused Bilal to renounce his belief. He had listened to Allah's Messenger for three days, learned about Allah Who had created everything out of nothing, and become came to know Him by His Messenger himself. After such a great blessing, no force could possibly pull him away from Allah and separate him from the way of his Lord. Neither torture, nor money, nor power or position, or anything else, could make him renounce his belief. This is what he did. Despite being subjected to unspeakable punishment, he proclaimed his belief to his last.

But this was only the beginning. The oppressors with not a shred of mercy in their hearts were not finished with him yet. Bilal could not have even imagined what they were going to do to him after this. For his heart had not become stone like theirs. In spite of his ordeal and all the difficulties he faced, he was as full of love as to forgive even those who exacted unconscionable cruelties against him.

One! One! One! Allah is One!

---

[10] Ibn Manzur, *Mukhtasar*, 5:204.

Bilal listened to each new revelation at every opportunity from the Messenger of Allah himself. As such, he had deepened in belief, had the veils of truth lifted, and seen what he needed to see. This is why the cruelties of the tyrannical Umayya and the Meccan street urchins he gathered around him could not have deterred him.

Umayya ibn Khalaf's heart was full of hatred and enmity and he enjoyed recruiting the idle Meccan youths and torturing the defenseless Muslims. He would frequently rally the idle city youth and go to the place they kept Bilal, with the mien of a hero saving the Meccans from a great calamity. When he got close to the door he instructed the boys to take Bilal out and tie a long rope around his neck. The youths around at the time would rush to gather round and watch what was happening. Once Bilal had been bound tightly and taken out

Umayya would order them to walk, dragging him through the city until they reached the place where they would torture him. The street urchins would treat the Prophet's Companion like a plaything, hurling insults at him, stoning and dragging him across the ground just for fun. When they finally reached the torture sight, Bilal al-Habashi did not have strength left to stand. As the youths had pulled on his rope so roughly, there would be cuts around his neck, and before his former wounds even had a chance to heal, everything got repeated all over again.

When he got to the point where he couldn't speak from the torture he was subjected to, or lost consciousness, the perpetrators would not leave him be. Instead, they took turns in their torment and abuse. More often than not, they would drag him all the way to the hills of Safa and Marwa, torturing him until they themselves grew weary from all the exertion, and subjecting him to every form of persecution imaginable to force him to renounce his religion. But they could not have succeeded no matter what they did. For this hero of belief in Divine Unity would never have conceded.[11]

Bilal's perseverance drove the Meccan polytheists out of their mind and drove them to forget their own humanity. They were rendered ineffectual in the face of his patience, perseverance, sincerity, straightforwardness, determination and resilience. They could only lunge at him in a state of murderous frenzy and continue their excruciating torture. Bilal did not have even strength enough to speak, merely uttering mournfully,

---

[11] Zarqani, *Sharh al-Mawahib*, 1:499; Ibn al-Athir, *Usd al-Ghaba*, 493.

"One! One! Allah is One!" He would call out to the idolaters that Allah was One, that their idols were not deities as they claimed them to be, and that Allah was the sole Being Who was worthy of worship.

Most of the time, Bilal was not alone. Other Companions would also be brought right next to him and subjected to similar acts of torture. One such Companion, Ammar ibn Yasir, was in admiration of Bilal's strength to endure all that befell him. He used to remember those days years later, saying of Bilal:

"The Meccans subjected us to the most excruciating of torture and, as such, would make all of us say what they wanted us to say, even if just with our tongue and not at heart. Only Bilal would not do so. They could not make him say anything he himself did not want to say."[12]

With not a shred of mercy left in his heart, Umayya ibn Khalaf grew petulant when he did not get want he wanted, seeking alternative ways of making his punishment more effectual. For instance, he used to wait for the sun to be at its zenith to bring Bilal, who had become a symbol of steadfastness and whom he had made a hero with his own doing, to his knees. On one such day the sun was at its highest point and had begun scorching everything under it. Sweltering from the intense heat, the people withdrew to their homes and there was no one around.

At an hour the city's inhabitants feared fainting from the heat and dared not go outside, the heartless Umayya did not hesitate to do so and gathered his men. As usual, he went straight to where they kept Bilal. After having him bound by the youth, they went outside all together and headed in the direction of the desert. Their brains were boiling from the heat and beads of sweat trickling down their faces. Paying no mind to this, they just kept dragging a defenseless person across the ground. Their hatred, enmity and anger made them willing to stand under the sizzling sun in the sweltering heat of the desert. In torturing Bilal, they were actually torturing themselves also and collapsed from exhaustion under the oppressive heat.

They took Bilal to the desert, dragging him as per usual, and lay him down on the burning sand. He felt an unbearable pain shoot through his body when his back made contact with the sand turned ember under the sun. Although gulping back the bitter anguish, he could not help but moan

---

[12] Ibn Sa'd, *Tabaqat*, 3:232; Suhayli, *Rawda al-Unf*, 2:84; Ibn Hajar, *Isaba*, 735.

from the pain. While he burned on the blazing sands, Umayya just came up beside him to listen to the deep mournful sounds Bilal uttered in agonizing pain. Umayya derived great pleasure from doing so, the painful cries stirring his inhumanity. He would indicate the large masses of rocks as searing as to burn the hand of any who touched it.

"Bring them here!" he would order his henchmen, getting them to put the stones that even several men carried with difficulty, on the chest of the Prophet's Companion. Bilal was crushed under.

"One! One! Allah is One!" he moaned.

His cries of Allah's unity would cause Umayya to flame with anger and the latter only intensified his torture. The scorching sun and thirst on the one hand, and on the other, the burning hot sand and a stone big and heavy enough to bury the Prophet's Companion into it.

As the sun blazed fiercely high in the sky, Bilal lapsed in and out of consciousness, and as his skin touched the smoldering sands, he wanted scream, to rent the skies asunder and shake the heavens and earth. But no matter the outcome, he didn't. So as not to give the Meccan polytheists any further satisfaction, he grit his teeth and merely moaned in suffering.

As the sun rose higher and higher, its severity of its heat intensified, turning the sands into burning ember. As these sands began melting Bilal's skin, Umayya's henchmen brought the rocks it took at least four of them to carry once again and placed them on his chest. Bilal grasped for breath and felt as though he was going to die. While he struggled for some time to endure the ordeal, he eventually fell exhausted and then unconscious. In spite of this, he continued to resist. Umayya flew into a fit of rage, standing above Bilal.

"Now," he began, without regard to the fact his victim had blacked out, "accept our idols and say that you've renounced Muhammad's religion!"

Great people are tested with great difficulties. History is replete with such examples. Bilal, too, was faced with a huge trial. But he had come to know Allah and had learned of His attributes from the Messenger of Allah himself. His heart brimmed with love of his Lord. Even as he was being tortured he was perpetually with Allah, in His Presence, and filled with love for Him. He would engage in contemplation of Him, mention Him, call upon Him for help, and seek refuge in only Him from the polytheists and all that they did to him. Without care for the punishment to which his persecutors subjected him, he constantly repeated, "One! One! Allah is One!"[13]

He had found his Lord and had become occupied exclusively with Him. All this persecution aside, even if his body were to be cut up into tiny pieces, like Habib ibn Zayd the hero or Yamama, he would still not care for the idols, and would continue to proclaim, "Allah is One."

The persecution and torture in Mecca was unabated, with one beginning when another ended. On another occasion, at a time when everyone suffered from heat exhaustion, and drank something and rushed to take shade in order to cool off, they did not give Bilal anything to drink for an entire twenty-four hours. Once he had gotten extremely thirsty, they shackled his ankles and took him to the desert once again, in their effort to get him to accept Lat and Uzza just once, even if only in word. Repeated attempts at doing so resulted in failure. They just could not accept this and tried over and over again. This occasion was no different. They took Bilal out to the desert to force him to profess his belief in the idols Lat and Uzza.

The weather was exceptionally hot, so much so that it seemed impossible to be outdoors at all. The trip to the desert was an ordeal in itself. When they got there, they were completely doused in sweat and their brains seemed to be boiling. They stripped Bilal replacing his clothes with a mesh iron coat used as armor, and lying him down on the sand. While the desert sun blazed on the one hand, there was the armor that the sun's rays heated and turned into a ball of fire on the other. This was not to be borne. With the extreme heat and thirst, Bilal faded in and out of consciousness. Not allowing for even this, the Meccan polytheists repeatedly doused him with water to bring him back and continue their torture. The Meccans standing around the unconscious Companion tried their utmost to get him to accept their idols and reject Islam, but to no avail.[14]

It made no difference to Bilal no matter what they did. For the light of belief shone so brightly in his heart during this torture that it would illuminate not only his heart but the hearts of those to come thousands of years after him also.

The shrouds of heedlessness faded away one by one in the face of the luminance of the Divine light. When the shrouds disappeared, Bilal al-

13 Ibn Sa'd, *Tabaqat*, 3:232; Ibn Abd al-Barr, *Isti'ab*, 1:179.
14 Ibn Sa'd, *Tabaqat*, 3:232; Dhahabi, *Siyar A'lam an-Nubala*, 1247.

Habashi saw the realm of meaning more clearly. Delving into this realm shown to him by his Lord, his entire being was filled with His love, and all his limbs and faculties pronounced His Name. The only thing they could get out of him no matter how hard they pushed and the intensity of their coercion, was "Allah is One."

These lofty words reached every inch of the universe and resounded in every corner. As indicated by Qastalani in his *Mawahib al-Ladunniyya*, by uniting so perfectly the agonizing pain of persecution and the savor of belief, Bilal al-Habashi reached the pinnacle of love.[15]

While the Meccans tortured him, he was together with his Lord. The universe disappeared, the world and all that it contains faded into nothingness, as though he was alone with his Lord. Was this not the case in reality?

Allah always exits.

He was One, eternal without beginning (*azal*), and eternal without end (*abad*).

It was only He Who was Everlasting, and was not everything going to perish anyway? Bilal al-Habashi experienced this in reality, dying before his death, and felt to his very core his Lord and his love for Him. At every act of torture, each time unbelief was pushed upon him, he experienced a state of ecstatic rapture spiritually, simply saying repeatedly,

"One! One! Allah is One!"

He was flinging his oppressors' wrongs, their associating partners with Allah, in their faces, in all its bareness. He was declaring that those idols that are not even aware of their own existence could not have creative capacity, and that the Being Who created the universe was One and Only One. He proclaimed to all humanity that *shirk* (speculating a partner to Allah) would be uprooted, exclaiming, "One, One! Allah is One!"

When the Meccan polytheists forced him to accept their idols, he immediately severed connection with the world and, by attaining the spiritual station of the "certainty of vision" (*ayn al-yaqin*), delved into remembrance of his Lord, bowing before Him with the reverence of as though seeing Him. Indicating that fortuitous moment when belief in his Lord enveloped every atom of his being, Bilal al-Habashi responded to

15 Zarqani, *Sharh al-Mawahib*, 1:499.

the idolaters who forced him to renounce his belief through torture with these profound words:

"Had I known any other word, I could not have borne this much torture and would surely have uttered it. My Lord is Allah. He is One. No matter what you do, my tongue will say nothing else."

One of those who witnessed the persecution of the Prophet's Companions was Amr ibn al-As, who was not yet Muslim. He could not forget what he saw despite this and would relate it years later as follows:

"I went to see Bilal al-Habashi. The Meccans had taken him to a place called Ramda, where they were torturing him. Had someone placed a piece of meat on the desert sands that day, the heat would have been enough to cook it immediately. But Bilal withstood the persecution, paying no mind to the heat. As the Meccans demanded, "Accept Lat and Uzza!" he constantly exclaimed, "I reject your your Lat and Uzza." Umayya's anger increased as Bilal said these words and Umayya increased the torture. When Bilal lost consciousness, they poured water on him only to would torture once more when he came to his senses."[16]

Bilal himself would narrate his experiences years later saying: "They used to leave me without food or water for a whole day and then take me to Ramda when the heat was most intense, where they would subject me to torture."[17]

[16] Ibn Sa'd, *Tabaqat*, 3:232; Baladhuri, *Ansab al-Ashraf*, 1:210.
[17] Baladhuri, *Ansab al-Ashraf*, 1:211.

CHAPTER 2

FREEDOM IN MECCA

THE FREEDOM THAT COMES WITH PATIENCE AND PERSEVERANCE

At a time when slaves were not seen as human beings, there was of course someone who esteemed Bilal al-Habashi and those like him, who cared for them and who concerned himself with their plight. This was none other than the ocean of compassion and mercy, the master of love, Prophet Muhammad, peace and blessings be upon him, himself. He was deeply grieved and hurt by the persecution Bilal and the others were subjected to, and felt their pain in his own heart. He made his support felt by being next to them, shared their pain, and constantly sought ways of putting an end to their persecution. When the torture became unendurable, he concerned himself even more so with them, going to see them at every opportunity, urging them to persevere, and constantly recommending patience and steadfastness. In doing so, he also simultaneously sought an answer to the question of how he could save them from the Meccan polytheists.

There was in fact something that could be done: buying them from their persecutors and setting them free. This could have been a way of ending their unceasing suffering. Upon deciding on the rightness of this course of action, he raised the matter on several occasions with Abu Bakr, one of the well-to-do Companions, encouraging him to help deliver Bilal al-Habashi and the other Companions from torture. He even suggested that they buy Bilal jointly.

Abu Bakr too was profoundly saddened by what was happening and had long been thinking about what he could do for them. The Messenger's discussing the issue with him and encouraging him in this way was enough to spur him into action. He went to Umayya ibn Khalaf. Umayya was preoccupied at the time with afflicting Bilal with great pain. Abu Bakr was concerned that Umayya would make trouble. He did not want to make things worse and so avoided directly stating his intention. He approached Umayya and greeted him.

"How resilient the man is!" he repined. "I daresay no amount of coercion will be of any use. For he will not say what you want him to say." Umayya was on the verge of giving up.

"You're right," he said. "So what should I do now? I am supposed to just let him go after all this effort?"

"If you want, you can sell him to me," Abu Bakr responded. "Can't you see he's going to die anyway if you torture him anymore? Then, he's not going to be of any use to you or to me. What is more, he would have become a hero at your own doing."

Umayya and the likes of him lost all ability to think logically when it came to money, and they just suddenly lost sight of their objective and mission. On top of that, some time ago, a figure whose views they held in high esteem had come to them just as they tortured Bilal with a word of warning:

"What are you doing?" he chided. If you kill him during torture, what you're trying to do will backfire. The people will take pity on him and direct their anger at you, turning him into a hero and visiting his grave."[18]

Umayya pondered on the truth of these words. What good would a slave that would die soon be to them anyway.

Taking all this into consideration, Umayya was convinced and began haggling over the price. Umayya sold Bilal for seventy *uqiyya*.[19] This was a steep price for a slave in his predicament. Abu Bakr would have paid any price to purchase Bilal, but his expression betrayed no emotion. Once the bargaining was over, he unbound Bilal's rope and took him straight home. He had a bed arranged for him and ensured that Bilal rested until the end of his treatment.

---

[18]   Suhayli, *Rawda al-Unf*, 2:89.
[19]   1 *uqiyya* is 1283 grams.

When Bilal regained consciousness and was on the way to recovery, Abu Bakr did Bilal a second kindness that he would never forget. He set him free.[20]

Approaching the age of forty at the time, Bilal could not believe that he had escaped the enslavement that had given him nothing but constant pain and dragged him from one affliction to another until this day. It took him a long time for him to recover from the effects of what he had been through. He experienced so many different emotions at the same time, his joy reflected in his eyes and face. Had it been possible for us to back in time, who knows all the things he would have had to tell us.

The polytheists were right. Sooner or later, the body of those whose heart and spirit had been liberated was freed from enslavement also. However, there was one very important fact that they had overlooked. Maybe one that they did not want to see... But anybody who looked just a little carefully could easily see it. The truth that surfaced once more time with Abu Bakr's suggestion was their superficial, token devotion to their idols and their beliefs. When the slightest personal advantage or money came into question, they readily abandoned their beliefs, principles and values, and hastened in the direction of their own interests.

They exerted themselves in the way of feeling no remorse or to avoid being shamed before those around them, taking care to cover up their insincerity. They glossed over their perfidy, presenting it to the people as virtue. After a while, they themselves believed their own lie and became the staunchest defenders of their wrongs. Seen in every individual who gives up their own human values, such a situation is a disease that is very difficult to treat.

The Qur'an describes the qualities of these people in various verses. One such verse palpably expresses just how weak is the cause of the unbelievers as is their commitment to their cause. As such, it emboldens the believers in their own struggle:

"Those who (truly) believe fight in Allah's cause, while those who disbelieve fight in the cause of taghut (powers of evil who institute patterns of rule in defiance of Allah). So (O believers), fight against the friends and allies of Satan. Assuredly, Satan's guile is ever-feeble" (4:76).

---

[20] Dhahabi, Siyar A'lam an-Nubala, 1247.

MERCY UPON MERCY

Who knows what they will go through in life?

What they will face and what they will be tested with.

Who can possibly know that while they are in their own world, they would be attacked, be enslaved and sold at market?

That their lives would be in the hands if another, that they would experience ordeal of every hue, and oppression and torture of every kind.

That they would be left all alone in distant lands, the names of which they had not even heard, and with their freedom and will be taken away from them, be condemned to pursue a strange existence.

Who could have known what wisdom lay behind all that had happened and all the gut-wrenching agony they had experienced?

That some things that were seemingly good were in actuality evil, and that some of those things that appeared evil were essentially good.

That the difficulties they faced actually lifted the curtains enabling them to see the reality that would lead them to perfection, were each a bounty, Divine-bestowed, to enable them to earn eternal happiness, and that the path to Paradise was paved with patiently enduring all difficulties.

Who could have known that afflictions were in reality mercy-laden clouds, that they would pour forth Allah's mercy by transforming the suffering gathered in those clouds into mercy?

That such times where trials and tribulations were actually experienced, when darkness congealed and set out to strangle a person, when hopes disappeared one by one, and where the curtains of heedlessness thickened, were in fact times to don discernment and see the wisdom connecting all these events.

After all, is not the psychological pressure caused by affliction one of the thickest screens obscuring vision of mercy?

The actual affliction is not the affliction itself. The real affliction is to be crushed beneath one's grief, is constant lamentation and remonstrance, and the failure to think about looking at the mercy behind the veil, or at the very least, to think about being hopeful. The failure to turn to Allah, the All-Merciful, and entreat Him for the opening of the doors of mercy, is to be dragged towards being one of those who lose. This is when the affliction really becomes affliction and becomes a true plague.

Happy are those who are patient during misfortune, who do not despair in their Lord and perceive it to be a test, even a Divine favor, and who raise the veil over their eyes, minds, and hearts to see the mercy behind!

From the moment Bilal al-Habashi first opened his eyes to the world; he was face-to-face with a grueling life. When he became a Muslim he was subjected to one persecution after another. His life constantly passed in patience and perseverance. When the torture reached unbearable dimensions, he submitted to his Lord and took refuge in the Unique One of Absolute Oneness (*Ahad*). Pleased with His servant, his Lord rewarded him in this world and in the Hereafter, elevating him to matchless spiritual ranks and stations.

Now he was being purchased by Abu Bakr. Unconscious during torture at the time, Bilal was perhaps not even aware of what was happening. After making the purchase, Abu Bakr brought Bilal back to his senses and took hold of the arm of the hero of patience who had no strength left to stand, bearing him up and almost dragging him all the way to his home. The Meccans, who had never before seen such a scene, were in utter astonishment as they stood staring at them in wonder.

One of the richest men in Mecca had purchased a dying slave, paying an excessive price, without a moment's hesitation. As if this weren't enough, he took him to his own home and lodged him in the most special space, treating his wounds with great care and tenderness. This was beyond belief. Nobody could believe their eyes. How was it that a person born and raised in a society which regarded addressing slaves abasement could see them as human just like himself, maintain that there was no difference between them, and pay the equivalent of a fortune for such a person?

The Meccans were utterly stupefied by what they saw. Even Abu Bakr's father Abu Quhafa, who was not yet Muslim, could not understand the situation. He was baffled when the news reached him. As he was not looking through the window of belief, he struggled to make sense of why his son did such a thing. Eventually, he could stand it no longer and intervened.

"Son! It seems that you are buying feeble slaves and emancipating them. If you are indeed so resolved to liberate them, then you might as well buy the strong ones and free them, for it may well be that one day they will protect you and fight for you when you so need it."[21]

Bilal received the special attention and care of Abu Bakr and his household and recovered in a short space of time. He got back on his feet and returned to daily life. Even if the traces of torture were still there, his pain had to a great extent disappeared. When Abu Bakr sat and talked with him once he had come through, telling him that he had manumitted him, Bilal could not believe his ears. Who knows all the things that occurred to his heart? How moved he was. What emotions he experienced we cannot know.

GLAD TIDINGS

Like Bilal al-Habashi, his mother Hamama was also a slave. Years ago, she had been forced to set out on an arduous journey. The oppressors who had taken her captive and bound her hands sold her at market like chattel and the masters who bought her to foreign lands, forcing her to walk across boundless deserts. While she was a slave who was not even given human status in the city of Mecca to which she was forcibly brought years prior, her suffering had transformed into a mercy without equal, through belief. She too had received a share of the mercy pouring forth from the heavens. When the Prophet of Mercy had called all humanity, free and slave, woman and man, to eternal Paradise, she responded to his call along with her children and attained everlasting felicity.

When her son came to her and related to her the sublime truths, a great fervor enveloped her heart. Knowing full well that danger of death at its end, she could not turn her back on the truths that were each more radiant than the Pleiades.

How could she have rejected the realities that reminded her of her own humanity?

Could she have turned a blind eye to the eternal bliss promised her, the Highest Paradise, and the bounties prepared for those who believe?

Eventually, she embraced Islam without a second thought, knowing that there was death at the end. It did not take long for the true face of the polytheists to be revealed once more. She was not mistaken. Insults, pressure, threats, and unbearable torture reared their ugly head.

---

[21] Shami, *Subul al-Huda*, 2:362.

She endured patiently, clinging to the Qur'anic verse, *"Surely Allah is with the persevering and patient"* (2:153). She knew for certain that even if she did not know whether or not she would die as a result of the torment and persecution, she would be admitted into Paradise if she was patient. For this is what her Lord promised the believers.

Her Lord's winds of mercy blew incessantly, just as they always had. There was Abu Bakr who only yesterday purchased her son Bilal and rescued him from the Meccan polytheists. Was there anything preventing her from having hope in her own deliverance? Why should she not be saved and gain her freedom, like her son? She was not wrong in hoping. Abu Bakr not only saved Bilal, but also bought and rescued his mother Hamama from the Meccan polytheists at the very first opportunity. He then set her free also.[22]

Referred to in the Qur'an as the condition of prospering in both worlds,[23] patience is a means to forgiveness, mercy, and guidance.[24] Because Allah is with the patient, patience attracts Allah's help. Because victories can only be won with His help, it has been said that good things come to those who wait.

It is thus time for reward and mercy for Hamama. She patiently endured the persecution she faced years ago, and put up with so many hardships. Her Lord showered her with His mercy and honored her with belief. She was to receive her share, in this world, of her Lord's promise of "reward without measure"[25] to those who are patient, by gaining her freedom.

ONGOING PERSECUTION

It is not just a de facto system of slavery that is applied directly in society. There is more an indirect slavery. This is because it is very difficult to maintain slavery directly, continuously and in widespread fashion, while virtually impossible in societies where people are conscious and informed. Such a situation makes it difficult for people who have an inexhaustible ambition. Such pitiful people, who have always wanted to enslave the people, see themselves as demigods in their delusions of grandeur, and

---

[22] Ibn Hajar, *Isaba*, 11049; Ibn al-Athir, *Usd al-Ghaba*, 6849; Maqrizi, *Imta al-Asma*, 1:36.
[23] See 3:200.
[24] See 2:157.
[25] See 39:10.

spend their lives for the sake of making slaves of humanity. The masses they cannot enslave directly, they set out to enslave in a roundabout way. They do this via a caste system in some societies, and a class system in others. In some societies, they oppress the poor, the forlorn, the weak and ordinary people by snubbing and holding them in contempt, and enslave them by subjecting them to physical, economic, social, and psychological pressure. They find a great many justifications for suppressing the people. Sometimes this is realized through thought or belief, sometimes via race or kindred, and sometimes through dress or lifestyle.

This was commonplace, even customary, for the Meccan polytheists. Wherever they saw a defenseless poor soul, they would walk all over them, assaulting their wealth and possessions and even their honor. Standing against those who engaged in such persecution and flinging their tyranny in their faces was not for the faint hearted. Those who showed such courage and conviction would either be silenced by those unfortunates oblivious to the fact that their turn would one day come, would be slighted, or would be lost amidst the dozens of meaningless words the rabble voiced in opposition.

For the truth to be heard, there needed to be either a strong voice, or as many people to come forward, declaring the oppressors to be oppressors, as could drown out the voices of those who stood against them. But it was very difficult for this many people to come together in a milieu characterized by intense social pressure. While people become inured to wrongs and come to view those who do good or who speak the truth with suspicion in such societies, those who engage in theft, insolence, oppression, and who suppress and despise those they view as the other are put on a pedestal. Those who are aware of the situation don't speak up, either in the name of their lives, property, interests, friendship, indifference, or for things not to get worse than they already are, or because they do not want any trouble.

There are always people who still have some goodness left in their hearts, or whose sense of justice is still alive and alert. Watching the unfolding of events with bated breath, they are troubled with the scene before them, and writhe under the pain of not being able to do anything or speak the truth. Meanwhile, the oppressors who exploit the plight of those who are suppressed and as good as enslaved perpetrate flagrant persecution while they have free rein.

When the Messenger of Allah was twenty years of age, in the month of Dhu al-Qa'da, a Yemeni man headed towards Mecca to sell his goods. As soon as he arrived in the city, he went straight to market. It was not long before he made his first sale. A Meccan by the name of Al-As ibn Wa'il offered to buy all his goods. With the haggling over, Al-As took the goods and attempted to leave without paying for the goods he had just purchased. The merchant struggled to recover his property, yelling and screaming. But it was clear from the outset that his actions were in vain. Al-As was used to seizing the goods of foreigners, and he had no intention of making payment for the goods he had just taken. The merchant could do nothing but writhe in agony for fear of his life. Al-As cared nothing for the man's grief and he took off as if nothing had happened.

The Yemenite had come regularly to Mecca for trade. He knew that Mecca's notables used to sit conversing in groups around the Ka'ba, and that those with a problem would appeal to them for help. Unable to get over the injustice he suffered, he hastened to the Ka'ba to ask for help. The Quraysh were in their usual meeting places.

"Al-As ibn Wa'il has refused to pay for the goods he purchased from me," he called out in his plea for assistance. "Please help me! Retrieve my goods or my money!"

In Meccan society at the time, people were enslaved to power, position, rank and money, and had sacrificed all their values for the sake of protecting what was in their possession. They had forgotten the concept of justice and had failed to realize that their turn would one day come also. As a result, they did not even listen to the man, let alone help him. They merely scolded him and tried to get rid of him. When the man insisted, they knocked him about. Seeing the deplorable state of the people of the Sacred Lands grieved him even more. But he had no intention of giving up. He was determined to fight to the end, even if it cost him his own life.

That night, he waited without doing anything. Early the next morning, he went to (Mount) Abu Qubays to have his voice heard by the people. By that time, members of the Quraysh had already begun sitting in circles around the Ka'ba. The man began yelling at the top of his voice, describing at length, and in verse, the injustices to which he had been subjected. He stated that what had been done to him was not at all befitting the guardians of the Ka'ba. The people of the Quraysh who attached great importance to honor and glory, were not impressed the man's words. They were angry not with the thief, the shameless, or the wrongdoer, but with the man himself.

It goes without saying that not all Meccans were of the same opinion. Even if small in number, there were individuals among them who had not lost their sense of truth and justice, and who listened to their conscience. One such figure was the Messenger's uncle Zubayr ibn Abdul Muttalib. He stood up.

"We can't turn a deaf ear to what this man is saying and just ignore him," he said. "We have to solve this problem right here, right now."

But the others did not think so, not seeing the injustice perpetrated as anything out of the ordinary. As they saw it, if those truth-loving people who cared about such notions as truth, rights and justice would just keep quiet and not intervene, the man would eventually give up and leave the city, and the problem would just solve itself. But they did not keep quiet.

Zubayr ibn Abdul Muttalib leaped up and went to personally call on a great many families, the Hashimites first and foremost. He found those like-minded individuals who could not tolerate injustice, and spoke to them one by one. They all agreed to gather in the house of Abdullah ibn Jud'an. One of the meeting's attendees was the then twenty-year-old Prophet Muhammad, may Allah bless him and grant him peace. Once everybody had eaten, one of them opened the discussion.

"Unimaginable injustices are being done to the people in these sacred lands, even during the sacred months. We need to do something as soon as possible." Another said something else, and then the others. In the end, they came to a common agreement.

"We will act as one in the interests of any person who has been treated unjustly, and we will continue our struggle against the wrongdoer until he gives the one who is wronged their rights."

They swore an oath to Allah, thus beginning the Alliance of the Virtuous, recorded in the annals of history as the *Hilf al-Fudul*. They went straight to Al-As ibn Wa'il first and said,

"Either give the man his goods, or his money." Seeing just how serious those disputing the matter with him were, Al-As returned the Yemeni merchant's goods without objection. Mentioning this alliance years later, the Messenger of Allah was to say:

"I was present during the alliance that was formed in the house of Abdullah ibn Jud'an, which was more preferable to me than (the finest) red camels. Were I invited to attend such a meeting after having received Prophethood, I would accept it."[26]

This was not what all there was to Meccan persecution. Their cruelty and tyranny was as widespread as to be regarded commonplace. One of their victims was a foreigner, a woman.

A man from Banu Khatham came to Mecca during the sacred months with the intention of performing the pilgrimage, bringing with him his beautiful daughter. She possessed a legendary beauty. A Meccan polytheist by the name of Nubayh ibn al-Hajjaj was taken by her at first sight and forcibly took her away from her father, with evil purpose.

"Is there no one to help us and save my daughter from this man!" the man cried out in desperation. Those hearing his cries told him to call on the Hilf al-Fudul for help. The man went to the Ka'ba and called out to the Hilf. Members of the confederate clans, in all likelihood including the Messenger of Allah himself also, immediately rushed to the Ka'ba. Drawing their swords, they said, "Here's the help that you have been expecting. Tell us what's happened."

"Nubayh took my daughter by force for an evil purpose," the man said. Alliance members assured the man that they would go immediately and rescue his daughter. Taking him along, they went straight to where he lived, and called out, "You know who we are and what we have come here for! Let the girl go at once!" Nubayh, who had made a habit out of insolence, said, "All right, but on one condition. I will let her leave in the morning if you let her stay with me for the night."

"No way!" they said and, well-armed, began their approach towards the door. Gripped by fear, the miscreant was left with no other option but to give up the girl. With his daughter restored to him, the joyous man praised the Alliance of the Virtuous in verse.[27]

While Bilal al-Habashi's emancipation in a milieu where injustice and oppression were seen as normal saved him from excruciating torture, it

---

[26] *Musnad*, 1:193; Bayhaqi, *Dala'il an-Nubuwwa*, 2:38; Hakim, *Mustadrak*, 2:220; Ibn Kathir, *Sira*, 1:128; Shami, *Subul al-Huda*, 2:154; Halabi, *Sira*, 1:192.

[27] Ibn Sa'd, *Tabaqat*, 1:128; Ya'qubi, *Tarikh al-Ya'qubi*, 2:12; Ibn al-Jawzi, *Muntazam*, 2:308; Ibn Kathir, *Bidaya*, 1:129; Maqrizi, *Imta al-Asma*, 1:18; Shami, *Subul al-Huda*, 2:154.

could not protect him from oppression and persecution. The Meccans were quick to confront him and the Muslims who were saved from enslavement like him. As such, they essayed to repress and intimidate them, destroy their identity and enslave their selfhood. In doing so they gave them the following message:

"Okay, we accept your freedom. Somebody has your bought and manumitted you. That may be, but this does not require you to be share equal status with us. Never can we be regarded your equal. We do not even want to be in the same environment and share the same space with you. We are a noble people, while you are ordinary people who were slaves until recently and who were even unaware of their humanity. Know your place!"

This was the point at which one either lost or was forced to lose their footing. These were the kinds of details precisely in which Satan's intrigues and deception lay hidden. His evil schemes were built on the foundation of these secret concoctions. That which drags people and society to disaster is despising and crushing the other, thinking nothing of their abilities, preventing them from proving them, and treating them as though they were not even human.

This, the Meccan polytheists had systematized. They were going to continue protecting, even developing their system. All their plans were foiled with the beginning of Islam's invitation. As Allah's Messenger and his Companions objected to the people's oppressing and looking down on one another, and as they asserted that human beings were equal and that not might, but right needed to be made a measure, the Meccans flew into a fit of rage. As they saw it, this was never going to happen. To make sure that this did not happen, they attacked Islam with all their might and mobilized to completely destroy it. They strove to prevent Islam's spread by torturing those like Bilal, Ammar and Amir. When they failed, they tried something else—something they had always done and would continue to do until the end of time: bringing their social status, affluence, authority and position to the fore and holding the people in contempt. Extending this to every facet of life, they ventured to enslave the people with respect to their identity and selfhood.

They hatched insidious plans, wanting to decoy the Muslims into a trap that would destroy their identity. Their decided aim was to put their scheme into action, step by step, and to turn the Muslims into a part of their system. In this way, just as the representatives of this same system continue to do across the globe today, and are regrettably to a great extent successful in doing, they then sought to nullify such principles of Islam as the following:

that all people were equal like the teeth on a comb;

that excellence was only with piety and righteousness;

and that each and every human being was an honorable creature. They thus sought to assimilate the Muslims into their prevailing system. They never missed an opportunity to do so. One incident pertaining to the plan they had begun to implement is related by Ibn Mas'ud as follows:

The Messenger of Allah was once sitting with Suhayb ibn Sinan, Bilal al-Habashi and Ammar ibn Yasir, when some chiefs of the Quraysh passed by. Seeing them, Allah's Messenger invited the Meccan nobles to join them. Disturbed by such an offer, they saw no harm in disclosing what was in their hearts.

"O Muhammad!" they said. "Are you serious about wanting us to sit down with these people? Are you indeed happy with them? Or do you shamelessly seek for us to follow them? Do you not know that we will never accept this? You had better turn them away, and we might then even follow you."

After patiently listening to the Meccans, Allah's Messenger said, "Never will I turn away the believers."

By forcing Allah's Messenger to drive away the Muslims with low socioeconomic status, they wanted to impose the idea that superiority was not through piety and righteousness, but through power and affluence. But they did not give up when they failed, only stepping up to another stage of their insidious plans. This time, they tried conceding some of their requests to reach their greater objective.

"Sit with whom you will otherwhile, but drive these people away when we come to see you," they said. "After we leave, you can resume keeping company with them if you so wish."

Allah's Messenger became very hopeful that they might become Muslim as he had so wanted for them to be honored with Islam, so he accepted their request. Just to be sure, the Meccans insisted on putting this in writing. Upon this, Allah revealed the following Qur'anic verse: "*And do not (in the hope of persuading the chieftains of the unbelievers) drive away any of those (poor believers of humble social standing) who, in the morning and afternoon, invoke their Lord, seeking His 'Face' (i.e., the meeting with Him hereafter and His eternal, good pleasure)"* (6:52).

Proceeding to assert that such a situation was an important test for humanity, Allah declared: *"And it is in this way that We try people through one another: so that they (who think that such things as wealth and social status are the means of superiority) say (of the believers who are poor and lacking in recognized social status): 'Are these the ones among us on whom Allah has bestowed His favor?' Does Allah not know best who are the thankful (who recognize the real source and bestower of every good thing one receives, and act accordingly)?"* (6:53)[28]

By means of this verse, Allah indicated that human beings are different by virtue of wealth, position and social standing, knowledge, intelligence and aptitude, and that these are each a means of trial, immediately thereafter stating that He Himself was the true owner of all the enumerated bounties. As such, He willed for human beings avoid arrogance and to pass the test by remembering the real bestower of bounty and showing gratitude to Him.

The disquiet of the Meccan leaders who witnessed the idea of slaves being human like themselves spreading a little more through society with each passing day also increased. This was something they could never accept and was a situation that would shake the very foundation of their established order. Failing to persuade Allah's Messenger directly, they took to doing so in a roundabout way. They raised the issue with his uncle Abu Talib, so that he could press upon his nephew. Ikrima ibn Abi Jahl narrates what happened on that day:

"A group of dignitaries of the Quraysh headed by Utba ibn Rabi'a and Shayba ibn Rabi'a once went to Abu Talib and said: 'Abu Talib, speak to your nephew Muhammad and tell him to drive the slaves and covenanted slaves away from him. They are the slaves and workers that we put to work. Such close proximity to them is not proper. There needs to be a certain distance between us. If they continue to gather around him in this way, they will soon begin to see themselves as equal to us, and we won't be able to find anybody to work for us.

---

[28]   Ibn Manzur, *Mukhtasar*, 11:114; Fakhr al-Din al-Razi, *Al-Tafsir al-Kabir*, 12:234.

Tell him to turn them away and assure him that if he does, he would have grown in estimation in our eyes, and we would be more inclined to listen to what he says.'

Abu Talib listened carefully to the delegation of the Quraysh and went straight to Allah's Messenger once they had left. He conveyed to the Messenger what they had said. Umar ibn al-Khattab who was also present, commented: 'O Messenger of Allah, why do you not do as they ask so that we may ascertain the truth of their words (and whether or not they will change their stance against you)?'

Revelation of the Qur'anic verse began even before Allah's Messenger had a chance to respond. By means of this verse, Allah warned His Messenger against neglecting such believers as Ammar, Bilal and Khabbab on the basis of the words of the Meccan polytheists, and commanded him to maintain his close concern for them. He also supported the weak believers through consolation.

"*Warn with this (the Qur'an) those who (whether they already have true belief or not yet) are fearful in their hearts because they will be raised from the dead and gathered to their Lord, that they have, apart from Him, no guardian and confidant, nor intercessor, so that they may keep from disobedience to Allah in reverence for Him and piety, and be protected against His punishment*" (6:51).

When Allah's Messenger recited the verse, Umar ibn al-Khattab rued his words and went straight to Allah's Messenger to apologize for what he had said."[29]

Allah's testing His servants in this way has always continued, and will do so until the end of time. Indeed, many similar incidents took place after years had gone by.

Bilal al-Habashi, Ammar ibn Yasir and Khabbab ibn al-Arat continued to remain in close proximity to the Messenger of Allah even after the Emigration to Medina, just like they had done in Mecca. When such newly-Muslim chieftains as Ghatafan leader Aqra ibn Habis and Uyayna ibn Hisn saw them around Allah's Messenger, they were as astonished as the Meccan chiefs, looking down on them because of their poverty. They belittled these Companions due to their failure to fully internalize the principles of Islam. They found it odd to see them sitting around Allah's Messenger

29 Alusi, *Ruh al-Ma'ani*, 5:231.

and were even angered by this. Unable to contain themselves in the end, they attempted to expel them from his company.

If they saw such Companions as Suhayb, Bilal, Ammar or Khabbab near Allah's Messenger when they went to see him, they tried to send them away with insult. In justifying their actions, they argued that a negative impression should not be given to delegations coming to the city from outside. Going a step further, they said to the Messenger of Allah:

"We ask that you grant us special assembly, that the Arabs may recognize our superiority. When the Arab delegations come to you, let them see us, for we are embarrassed to be seen sitting with these slaves. So, when we come to you, send them away, then when we have finished, sit with them if you wish." In so doing, they sought privilege and special status exactly as the Meccan polytheists had done in the past.

Even the Messenger's listening and paying regard to these words, which were an insult to those Muslims with low social standing and weak economically, was enough for Divine admonition. Allah informed the Messenger exactly how he ought to treat them, commanding, *"When those who believe in all of Our Revelations and signs (whenever they come to them,) come to you, say in welcome: 'Peace be upon you!'"* (6:54).

Following this admonition, Allah's Messenger was even more particular when it came to the kindness and courtesy shown to Bilal al-Habashi and his friends, letting them sit as so close to him that their knees touched his.[30]

Khabbab ibn al-Arat, the narrator of the Prophetic Tradition, says: "(After this) we used to sit with the Messenger of Allah, and when the likes of Aqra and Uyayna were going to sit with Allah's Messenger, we would get up and leave (so that they would not look down on us and face ruin). When they left, we would return to sit with the Messenger of Allah."[31]

On the one hand were those who looked down on the people with disdain, relying on their economic strength and social status, while on the other were those heroes of belief who did not want the destruction of the believers who slipped and fell due to their inclination to the world.

On the one hand were the likes of Aqra and Uyayna who failed to fully interiorize the essence of belief and could not even stand to see the Mes-

30   Ibn Manzur, *Mukhtasar*, 11:115.
31   Ibn Majah, Zuhd, 7; Suyuti, *Al-Durr al-Manthur*, 3:248.

senger of Allah side-by-side with those poorer Muslims. On the other hand were the Bilals, Khabbabs, Amirs and Suhaybs who chanced moving away from the Messenger of Allah they held so dear, so that those who held them in contempt would not be destroyed.

This had to have been the summit of belief fellowship, of a consciousness of the rights of such fellowship. Being able to be like the noble Companions, striving to emulate them... Only as the dome of the firmament is illuminated by such precious stars, and their lives be held up as an example can humanity attain peace and tranquility.

THE WORTHIEST BEFORE GOD

One of the most important principles of Islam is for human beings to be servants not to one another, but to Allah alone. One of the key premises for this belief to take root in the heart is no doubt to accept, not in word but in one's heart, the principle that all people are equal.

Just as any particular race or ethnicity is not superior to any other race or ethnicity, wealth, intelligence, rank or position, and cultivation can never be cause for superiority and eternal happiness. Favorable conditions conferred upon human beings like money, intelligence, authority and knowledge can only be pluses when they are used correctly and when they lead a person to piety and righteousness. Else, when they are used as an excuse to look down on other people, as a means for self-conceit, scorning and crushing others, as a cause for violating the rights of and repressing others, they serve no other purpose other than causing the destruction of the human being both in this world and in the Hereafter.

At the beginning of the Messenger's open invitation to Islam, in those particular temporal and geographical conditions, people regarded wealth, affiliation with a great tribe, and status and position as a means of superiority. They exploited such an understanding to hold other people in contempt and deem themselves superior to them. Allah taught the community of Islam with the revelation He sent down, and by struggling against such deep-seated social diseases, He uprooted erroneous understandings one by one. When the occasion called for it, He warned his Messenger and indicated the consequence of the issue. One such occasion arose in Mecca.

As Allah's Messenger was once speaking with leaders of the Quraysh tribe, telling them about Islam, Ibn Umm Maktum approached him and asked him a question. At the time, Allah's Messenger preached with great fervor and was exerting utmost effort for the people of the Quraysh to accept Islam, and was disturbed by the interruption of another person right at that point. But because Ibn Umm Maktum was blind, he was not aware of what was happening. He persistently continued asking questions. Seeing his insistence, it never even occurred to Allah's Messenger to get angry with or reprimand him. He merely frowned slightly and turned away.

Allah did not want him to show even this much response, and warning His Messenger and all Muslims to come until the Day of Judgment through his person, He declared, *"He frowned and turned away, because the blind man approached him. What would inform you but that he might grow in purity (by doing good deeds)? Or that he might grow mindful (of Allah's Message), and the reminder benefit him?"* (80:1–4).

The verse expressly stated that just as there was to be no discrimination in bringing material service to human beings, there could be no discrimination in bringing them spiritual service. The verse stressed that the caller needed to consider not the people's (social or economic) status when addressing them, but at their petitions.

Allah and His Messenger state at every opportunity that no one is superior to another, that honor and excellence is only through goodness and righteousness, and that this honor could only be attained by adhering to His commands and prohibitions. This is why they did not look with favor on certain people being condemned to insignificance or inferiority. They waged a constant struggle to prevent such people being looked down on and treated wrongfully. To this end, they warned the Companions frequently, educating them and encouraging them to root out attitudes and perceptions that were a holdover from the Age of Ignorance.

Once, a certain Qays ibn Mutatiya came to Medina and when he saw Allah's Messenger seated with a group in which Suhayb ibn Sinan, Bilal al-Habashi and Salman al-Farsi were present, he was taken aback. He found odd the Messenger's keeping foreign company.

"The Arabs of the Aws and the Khazraj have stood up in defense of this man (Muhammad)," he muttered to himself. "But what are these people doing with him?"

Mu'adh ibn Jabal, who overheard him, was greatly disturbed by what he heard and immediately lay hold of him, taking him to the Messenger of Allah himself. Informing Allah's Messenger of what Qays had said, he voiced his complaint about the man. Angered by what he heard from Mu'adh, the Messenger of Allah rose and went straight to the mosque without speaking a single word. He instructed Bilal to recite the call to Prayer was given (as a means of summoning the believers for an important announcement). When his Companions gathered he stood up, took his place at the pulpit, praised and glorified Allah and said:

"O people, Your Lord is One. Your ancestor is one. Your religion is one. Take heed. Arabism is not conferred upon any of you through your mother or your father. It is merely through the tongue (i.e., the Arabic language), so whoever speaks Arabic, he is an Arab (and has no superiority by virtue of this)."

Confident in the rightness of his action, Mu'adh stood up, seized the man by his collar, and said, "O Messenger of Allah, what do you say about this hypocrite?" Allah's Messenger made no comment, only instructing Mu'adh to let the man go.[32]

The Arabs, who placed great importance on lineage and ancestry, were not easily able to free themselves of this. This disease was reflected in their human relations, marriage, and social life. Confronting Bilal al-Habashi, too, from time to time, it plagued him also. On one occasion, Abu Dharr who got angry at Bilal called him, "Son of a black woman." Grieved by the words of his friend, Bilal went to Allah's Messenger and related all that had happened between them. Allah's Messenger was disturbed by Abu Dharr's words.

Unaware that Bilal had complained to the Messenger of Allah, Abu Dharr came to the mosque and was not shown the same regard by Allah's Messenger as he had received until that day. This worried him.

"O Messenger of Allah," he said, "Do you turn away from me because of something you have been told?"

Allah's Messenger replied, "Have you reproached Bilal by reason of his mother? By the One who revealed the Book to Muhammad, no one is more superior to another except in deeds of righteousness."[33]

---

[32] Ibn Manzur, *Mukhtasar*, 11:117.
[33] Ibn Manzur, *Mukhtasar*, 5:262.

Many years passed and the people had come a long way on account of Islam. But despite all this progress, they could not fully free themselves of the attitudes of the days of ignorance. Awake to the importance of the matter, the Caliphs succeeding Allah's Messenger struggled against these attitudes and strove to prevent the people's enslavement of one another. They worked to prevent a relapse into the former state of disease.

One account attributed to Hasan al-Basri is reported as follows:

"A group of Muslims including Suhayl ibn Amr, Abu Sufyan ibn Harb and elder members of the Quraysh went to visit Umar. His doorman met them and ushered them into the waiting room. Suhayl ibn Sinan, Bilal al-Habashi, Ammar ibn Yasir, and other freed slaves who participated in the Battle of Badr were also there. They, too, were waiting for an audience with Umar. Taking into consideration their earlier arrival, the doorman gave them priority, and led them into Umar's presence. The leaders of the Quraysh deemed this strange, evincing their displeasure. Noticing their reaction, the doorman said, "By Allah, Umar was one of those who took part in the Battle of Badr and loves those who took part also. He informed me on the matter and instructed me to act accordingly." Listening with anger, Abu Sufyan bridled, "I have never met with such a thing! What is this! Saves such as these are given permission to enter while we nobles have been left at the door, and the doorman will not even attend to us."

Suhayl ibn Amr was troubled by his friend's words. Turning to Abu Sufyan, he said, "O people, I see your anger in your faces, but if you are to be angry, be angry at yourselves. You were invited to Islam as were they. They hastened to accept and you tarried.

By Allah, The virtue and excellence they have attained through the sacrifices they made in the way of Islam before you far outweighs the honor and virtue you now speak of. They surpass you in virtue and theirs is a degree you can never attain. Better to accept it."[34]

PROCESS OF SPIRITUAL BUILDING

From the moment he embraced Islam, his mind, heart and spirit illuminated, Bilal al-Habashi's life took on an entirely new meaning. Looking at people, nature and events in the Name of and for Allah, and insightfully, from the perspective at which Allah commanded him to do so, he saw fur-

---

[34] Hakim, *Mustadrak*, 3:282.

ther than the realms beyond, and even farther than that. He approached life with the light of belief and wisdom, evaluating it from the perspective of a believer and acted accordingly.

From the moment Abu Bakr emancipated him and his mother and provided him with a home and employ, he understood what was meant by freedom. Deciding for himself when he would get up and go to sleep, what he would or would not do, and how he would conduct himself, using his own volition as he saw fit allowed him to experience a sense of what it was to be human.

He was well aware that there was much to learn. Thus, paying no mind to the physical and psychological pressures of the Meccan polytheists, he strove to make the best use of his time. Like all the other Companions, his greatest desire was to learn, as soon as possible, the verses that were revealed to the Messenger of Allah. The first thing that came to his mind upon waking was to learn the Divine message that Allah sent to humanity, and by wiping away the wrongs in his subconscious through it, to give new shape to his belief, his view of life, and his thoughts and feelings in the light of the Qur'an. The most pressing problem preoccupying his thoughts was how to enter and leave what was for the Companions the most distinguished school of humanity, the House of Arqam, without getting caught by the Meccans. Those days he managed to do so, he considered himself the world's most fortunate person.

He would usually go there in the morning and be there till nightfall, when everyone has retired to their homes. He would memorize the newly-revealed Qur'anic verses and through reflection on the meaning of these verses, try to understand exactly what his Lord expected from him. Listening eagerly and carefully to the Messenger's explanations of the verses, he would be enlightened at heart and spirit. When night fell, he would sneak out with the same conscientiousness, returning to his home without being seen by anyone.

The Messenger of Allah turned the residence of Arqam ibn Abi al-Arqam, which he termed *Dar al-Arqam*, or the House of Arqam, into the finest school of humanity for his Companions. The Companions who came here at every opportunity would become acquainted with Allah through His Names and Attributes, and learn one by one the principles of belief and morality, the commandments and prohibitions, a person's relationship to Allah and His Messenger, other people and their own inner world, as well as learning about the former Prophets, their communities, and their monotheistic struggle. They would note in their minds and hearts the character traits that were requisite for a righteous person and take on the morality of the Qur'an and Allah's Messenger by translating these characteristics into action in their day-to-day lives.

It was on exactly such a day, when Bilal al-Habashi, filled with the fervor of learning the most recent revelation, wondered about the universal messages that his Lord had sent to humanity. He did not sleep after offering his late Night Prayers. He could not wait for morning. He left home early. Furtively, he began walking towards the House of Arqam, praying to Allah all along. When he finally reached the house, he made sure there was nobody else around and then rushed to the house's entrance. He lightly knocked on the door and entered when another one of the Companions opened it. Upon seeing the luminous, smiling countenance of Allah's Messenger and receiving the gaze that penetrated hearts and enkindled Divine love, his heart was filled with peace.

The Qur'anic chapter entitled Qaf that he learned with great excitement, love and enthusiasm, he would never forget for the rest of his life. After all his Companions had gathered, Allah's Messenger began his words, reciting the new revelation after a brief description.

The chapter put forth explicitly and fulfillingly, in a manner allowing for the words of no other, all the facets of belief in Allah. It encapsulated all that happened and was to happen from the creation of the human being until the end of time, took up the issues of belief in the angels, Divine Unity and Prophethood, described Allah with His Perfected attributes and proclaimed Him absolutely exalted above all deficiency and imperfection.

There was also an emphasis on the Messenger's mission as a warner. Wrong were unfurled for right to be understood, the veils concealing truth were lifted one by one as falsehood came to light, and truths unfolded in all their clarity.

The verses stressed the need for the removal of the obstacles on the path in order to reach that long-awaited good, as well as the disasters in store when truth and justice was ignored and disregarded. They also elucidated the opposition of the unbelievers to the Messenger of particularly, and all other Prophets in general, and described the reasons and consequences of this opposition. The unbelievers' objections were being confuted one by one through the Qur'an's matchless exposition. Also related through this means was the creation of many things, from the universe to the human being, death and life after death, the resurrection after death, the end of the world, the Hereafter and events to take place there.

After pointing to humanity being known best by Allah Who created them, the chapter describes His being closer to the human being than their jugular vein, explains to the Messenger, and through his person to all Muslims, the methods of inviting others to Islam, makes lucid the characteristics of those who believe and those who do not believe, and offers examples of scenes they were to encounter in the Hereafter.

"Qaf. By the Qur'an most sublime. (We have indeed, in spite of what they say, sent it to you to warn people that they will be raised from the dead to account for their lives)" (50:1).

The unbelievers showed deferential regard and attached great importance to the Qur'an in the Messenger's person. Despite their vehement opposition to the religion he conveyed, they did not hesitate to express the honor of the Qur'anic revelation, and in spite of their hatred and aversion to the truths that it proclaimed, they did not hide their admiration for it. What is more, even the Abu Jahls, the Umayya ibn Khalafs, and the Akhnas ibn Shariqs of the day who carried the banner for open hostility to Islam and exerted incredible pressure on society, secretly listened to it; upon being witness to its literary aspect, its eloquence, the magnificent inimitability in its words and sentences, the profundity and cogency in its meaning, and the lucidity of fluency in its style, there were virtually stupefied. Neither any ordinary Arab, nor the great masters of language hesitated to admit this. They readily understood its being the Divine word and did not hide their deference to it.

One of the other things that could not help but admit was their trust and confidence in Allah's Messenger. The Meccans who knew him very well openly spoke of his honesty, truthfulness, and trustworthiness, and praised his morality. When he informed them of his Prophethood and that he was a Messenger sent to them by Allah, they were shocked. These words, which they had not heard for centuries or which they heard from a distance, was the very last thing they could ever have wanted to hear. If somebody else had said this, they would have taken no notice, merely shrugging it off as the ravings of a madman. Or, as they had done to the likes of Waraqa ibn Nawfal, they would have minded their own business and left the owner of these words alone with their declamations. When the utterer of these words was one they had nicknamed *Al-Amin*, the Trustworthy, one who was the epitome of laudable conduct, they stopped and listened, and took him very seriously. Each verse was too perfect to have been the words of any mortal. As they listened, their wonderment increased. They were shaken up. What was being said was true, and yet would disrupt their established order and run contrary to the interests of their leaders. For this reason, they denied it, suppressing their emotion and reason. When they were unable to defend it, they grew aggressive, and instead of accepting the truth, took to doing the following:

"But they deem it strange that a warner from among them has come to them, and the unbelievers say: 'This is something strange!'" (50:2).

They chose the path of denial by producing irrational excuses. The reason for their reactions was never the Messenger's person or the Qur'an, but their particular situation and context, their social and political views.

Another reason was ignorance. It had been a long time since they had lost their ability to look at their surroundings with an eye to take lesson, to think, and to see the truth. Instead of trying to understand the truth, however, they tried to find fault. This, they did, in their own way. As they saw it, a person could not have been a Messenger of Allah.

Asserting, *"Has Allah sent a mortal man as the Messenger?"* (17:94), they deemed strange the Messenger's saying, "I am a Messenger of Allah" and turned against him.

For these people, with a corrupted thought systematics, an ordinary human being like them could not possibly communicate with Allah. Thus, they objected, saying, *"What sort of Messenger is this? He eats food and goes about in marketplaces (like any other mortal)"* (25:7).

Whereas had they paid just a little attention to knowledge and learning, they could have readily learned from the Christian and Jewish friends they saw frequently on their trade journeys that all Prophets and Messengers sent to humanity were actually human.

The second reason was deviation from the course of revelation. Hundreds of years ago, they had severed their connection with Allah and began pursuing their carnal desires and Satan himself. Over time, their nature became corrupted and their standards and value judgments disappeared. They reached the point where they could no longer think straight or see the truth for what it was. Just like in this matter, they looked at events from all the wrong vantage points. They could not even understand the vital wisdom behind a human's being sent as a Messenger. As per their skewed logic, if Allah had wanted to send a Messenger, He would have either directly sent an angel, or made an angel a means to the Messenger. Looking at the situation from the wrong window, the unbelievers criticized the Messenger of Allah on the street and at the marketplace: "*Why has not an angel been sent down on him?*" (6:8).

By saying such things as, "*Why is an angel not sent down to him so that he may act as a warner in his company (and help him to persuade the people)?*" (25:7) they worked to keep the people away from him.

The third reason was the dominant powers who held the people in contempt and those who were influenced by them. Dominant powers forever look at life and events from the window of their own imagined strength, power, egocentrism, and self-interest. They oppose anything that fell afoul with their own interests, without looking at whether it was right or wrong. Allah reproaches this tendency of theirs as follows:

"*Is it (ever so) that whenever a Messenger comes to you with what (as a message and commandments) does not suit your selves, you grow arrogant, denying some of them (the Messengers) and killing others?*" (2:87).

Perturbed at the thought of losing the people they controlled at will, these powers initiate an onslaught of denial and defamation:

"When Our Revelations clear as evidence and in meaning are recited to them (the Meccan polytheists), they say: 'This is but a man who wants to bar you from what your forefathers used to worship.' They also say (of the Qur'an): '*This is nothing but a fabrication falsely attributed to Allah.*' *Those who disbelieve say of the truth when it has reached them (in willful defiance of its clarity): 'This is clearly nothing but sorcery*' (34:43).

The unbelievers who supposed that the wealthy, those in authority, the leading powerful were first and foremost worthy of all things good did not see Prophethood as befitting Allah's Messenger. With a view to making his followers renounce their religion, they said, in their attempt at dissuasion:

"'*Why is a treasure not cast down upon him from the heaven (so that he should no longer need to go about in market-places to earn a living)?' Or: 'Why does he not have a garden (granted to him miraculously) to obtain his food from?' And so these wrongdoers say (to the believers): 'You are follow-ing only a man bewitched!'"* (25:8).

Putting aside reason and logic, they acted upon their prejudice. Rather than investigating the truth of the matter, or applying to their mind and reason, they accepted their bygone subconscious accumulations as a measure, to which they blindly clung:

"When it is said to them (who follow in the footsteps of Satan), 'Follow what Allah has sent down,' they respond: 'No, but we follow that (the tradi-tions, customs, beliefs, and practices) which we found our forefathers in'" (2:170).

When Ubayy ibn Khalaf heard the verses describing the resurrection of the human being after death, he grabbed a dry bone in his hand and went straight to Allah's Messenger. Crumbling the bone between his fin-gers and scattering the fragments in face of Allah's Messenger, he said, mockingly, "Muhammad, so you claim that Allah will bring me back to life after I have died and become dust and bones, like so? Is this what you believe also?" Showing utmost confidence and poise, Allah's Messenger said, "Yes, Allah, Who will cause you to die, will resurrect you and then gather you into the Fire." The following verse was thereafter revealed: *"And he coins a comparison for Us, having forgotten his own origin and cre-ation, saying, 'Who will give life to these bones when they have rotten away?'"* (36:78)[35]

Having long forgotten how to look with the eye of reason and take les-son, these people had become accustomed to looking merely with the eyes on their head. For this reason, they held blindly to their prejudices, their subconscious accumulations and the understanding they inherited from their forebears, and unmindfully opposed the words of Allah's Mes-senger, saying: *"When we have died and become dust (you say, we will be raised from the dead)? That is a far-fetched return!"* (50:3). Informing them of the erroneousness of their understanding, Allah addressed the question of resurrection in various chapters and answered their claims one by one.[36]

The real wonder was the situation of the unbelievers. They acted with-out certain knowledge, on the basis of their prejudices and the false infor-mation filling their subconscious, and were not even aware that this pre-

---

[35] Ibn Ashur, *Tafsir at-Tahrir wa at-Tanwir*, 26:282.
[36] See (36:78–79, 81); (18:4); (75:4); (22:6); (23:115–116); and (45:21).

vented their seeing the truth. Had they thought with a clear head for not long, for even just a short time, they could have understood the truth. But instead of facing reality, they chose to accuse the Prophet of Islam. Allah, Who rendered everything in the universe proof of His existence, His unity, as well as the life of the Hereafter, did not punish the unbelievers who insisted on not seeing these. He merely made clear to them the error of their ways and invited them to reflect:

"We know for certain whatever the earth corrodes of them (to the most minute particle); with Us there is a book recording and preserving (incorruptibly)" (50:4).

"Rather, they have denied the truth when it has come to them (and done so willfully and persistently), so they are in a dire state (utterly confused about how to explain their rejection, and about how to prevent the acceptance of others)" (50:5).

"But do they, then, never observe the sky above them (to ponder Our Knowledge and Power; and reflect) how We have constructed it and adorned it, and that there are no rifts in it?" (50:6).

The Messenger of Allah recited the chapter entitled Qaf again and again. Listening to him carefully each and every time, Bilal al-Habashi reflected upon the meaning of its verses. In each verse he saw Allah's infinite strength and power, His mercy and compassion. He perceived an unequalled Creator and All-Fashioning One and came to realize an incessant, torrential downpour of grace and favor. Maybe he even asked himself why, despite having constantly witnessed what was being related in the verses, he did not reflect upon what he saw until now. While he was preoccupied with such thoughts, the Messenger of Allah was reciting the sixteenth verse: *"Assuredly, it is We Who have created human, and We know what suggestions his soul makes to him. We are nearer to him than his jugular vein"* (50:16).

Bilal Al-Habashi was shaken when he heard this verse. Allah Who created the human being of course knew him better than he knew his own self. He knew his thoughts and feelings, what he did, and all that occurred to his mind and heart better than he did. He saw him at each instant, and knew his each and every state, moment to moment. He was ashamed for having turned his back on Allah for all these years and having worshipped idols made of wood and stone instead. Allah's Messenger expanded on the verse with an example:

"When one of Allah's servants rises in the morning, they stand in His presence. When they turn to their right and left, their Lord says to them, 'Where do you direct your gaze? To someone better than me? Know well that when the children of Adam turn to Me, I am the best of those to look upon them.'"[1]

Bilal thought at length at his being under the watchful gaze of Allah. Everything, from his actions and his thoughts and feelings, to the desires of his carnal self, were under control. This meant that he would be called to account for his actions. Where and how he led his life, what he did, or what he neglected doing would all be asked one by one.

It was Allah Who knew best his fears and hopes, his sincerity and wholeheartedness, all that he did that was marked with pretense, his love and reverence, his hatred and loathing, his turning to Allah, and his growing distant to Him. Allah, Who is closer to a person than their jugular vein, knows their pain and suffering, their grief and sorrow, and sees their happiness and rejoicing. Hearing both their supplication to be delivered from their hardship, grief and sorrow and their heart's entreaty, He responds to their plea. He rewards their praise and thankfulness by increasing His favor upon them.

Allah's nearness to His servant is, of course, not merely an intellective one. He is also near His servants with His love, His mercy and compassion, His grace and favor, His good pleasure and approval, and through His responding to them when they call on Him.[2]

"And when (O Messenger) My servants ask you about Me, then surely I am near: I answer the prayer of the suppliant when he prays to Me. So let them respond to My call (without hesitation), and believe and trust in Me (in the way required of them), so that they may be guided to spiritual and intellectual excellence and right conduct." (2:186).

One of the most important trials for the human being is evil suggestions and whisperings. Addressing this question in the Qur'an, Allah indicates the need for a person to gird consciousness of being forever under the Divine gaze to be able to deal with fear, worry, negative thought and feeling, baseless misgiving and delusion. He encourages the human being to worship Him and lead their day-to-day lives as though they were seeing Him. In order for them to reach a consciousness of being under His

---

[1]   Al-Tha'labi, *Al-Kashf wa'l-Bayan*, 7:38; al-Hindi, *Kanz al-Ummal*, 7:505.
[2]   Elmalılı Hamdi Yazır, *Hak Dini Kur'an Dili*, 6:4513.

constant supervision and to internalize a culture of self-supervision by abandoning heedlessness, He reminds them that He sees and hears them at every moment, though they do not see Him, and that He knows what occurs to their hearts, stating that He is closer to them than their jugular vein. He reminds them that their each and every step is recorded by the angels:

"Remember that the two recording angels (appointed to record his speech and deeds), seated on the right and on the left, receive and record." (50:17) *"Not a word does he utter but there is a watcher by him, ever-present."* (50:18).

After reciting the eighteenth verse, the Messenger of Allah paused for a short time; in order to point to the need for consciousness of being under Allah's watchful gaze to lead a person to self-criticism and then to repentance, he said: "All the words uttered by the children of Adam are recorded. Thus, the person who has erred must repent immediately, entreating Allah saying, 'My Lord, I seek Your forgiveness for the wrong I have committed and resolve never to repeat it.' If they do so, they will be forgiven so long as they do not return to their error."[3]

He then referred to two important principles and rules for avoiding frequent erring: "Let whoever believes in Allah and the Last Day either speak good or keep silent.[4] The excellence of one's Islam is their leaving that which does not concern them."[5]

He also stressed the unparalleled reward such an awareness would endow an individual with, and the calamity awaiting one who makes no effort to free themselves from heedlessness.

"One of you may utter a word that pleases Allah, unaware of how highly it will be regarded, and on its account Allah records for them His Good Pleasure until the Day they meet Him. One of you may utter a word that draws the anger of Allah, and not know how far it reaches, and on its account Allah records against them His anger, until the Day they meet Him." The narrator, Alqama, then said: "How many words I refrained from uttering on account of this Tradition."[6]

[3] Hakim, *Mustadrak*, 1:129; Tha'alibi, *Tafsir al-Tha'alibi*, 5:284.
[4] Hakim, *Mustadrak*, 1:129; Tha'alibi, *Tafsir al-Tha'alibi*, 5:284.
[5] Tirmidhi, Zuhd, 2317; Ibn Majah, Fitan, 3976; *Musnad*, 1:201; Tha'alibi, *Tafsir al-Tha'alibi*, 5:284.
[6] Bukhari, Riqaq, 6478; Tirmidhi, 2319; Ibn Majah, Fitan, 3970; *Musnad*, 3:469; Ibn Kathir, Tafsir, 7:277.

The Messenger of Allah continued reciting the chapter. Vividly depicting what would happen in the Hereafter, the verses contained within it strengthened Bilal and his friends' belief and consciousness in the Resurrection and Hereafter.

THE NIGHT VIGIL

From the moment Bilal al-Habashi, who received his instruction at the House of Arqam, first heard the Qur'anic chapter al-Muzzammil, he became one of the brightest stars of the luminous nights. He would wake in the silence that enveloped the night, at the point where sleep was sweetest. After taking ablution while reciting his supplication, he would turn to his Lord in deep reverence, and worship Him as though he were seeing Him. Abu Qatada narrates:

"The Messenger of Allah went out at night and found Abu Bakr praying in a low voice, passed Umar ibn al-Khattab who was raising his voice during the Prayer, and saw Bilal al-Habashi observing his Prayer in devoted reverence. After watching them for a while from a distance, he continued on his way. When he saw them the following morning, he said: 'I passed by you, O Abu Bakr, when you were praying in a low voice.'

Abu Bakr replied, 'O Messenger of Allah, I was heard by He whom I was addressing.'

The Messenger of Allah said, 'Raise your voice a little.' He then turned to Umar and said, 'You were praying in a loud voice when I passed by you.'

Umar replied: "O Messenger of Allah, I was awakening the drowsy and driving Satan away.'

The Messenger of Allah said to Umar: 'Lower your voice a little.' He then turned to Bilal and said, 'I saw you also. You were reciting from such to such-and-such chapter. All of you were correct."[7]

FELLOWSHIP IN MECCA

Fellowship is an innate emotion, a Divine favor, a heavenly bestowal, and a sacred mystery filled with miracles bringing hearts together. The way to being honored with this miraculous mystery is to set off with a sincere

---

[7] Abu Dawud, Tatawwu, 25; Ibn Manzur, *Mukhtasar*, 13:267.

intention, embrace those who believe in Allah purely for His sake and without any other consideration, and to receive them not self-seekingly, but wholeheartedly. It is to shed all thought of personal advantage, gain and petty interest, and to don the garb of self-sacrifice.

Fellowship is an incomparable process of building and discipline. It entails casting such evil feeling as arrogance, pride, hatred, animosity and jealously into the melting pot of trust and self-sacrifice, and becoming not an Abu Jahl or Abu Lahab, but an Abu Bakr or Umar. The Messenger of Allah describes those who embrace one another in all sincerity as follows:

"The believers in their mutual affection, mercy, and compassion, are like a single body; if one limb aches, the rest of the body reacts with sleeplessness and fever."[8]

When a believer meets with their fellow believer, they put their rank, position, and own interests aside. They do not even expect a thank you for their help, devotion and self-sacrifice. Earning the good pleasure and approval of Allah is enough for them. Even if they see evil in return, they do not change their stance.

Fellowship is to abandon producing such artificial values as supremacy of race, tribe, profession, or sect, and ascribing sanctity to these. It is to discard the dregs of Ignorance, to purify ourselves of hatred, enmity and jealousy, and to thus find peace.[9]

Deeply grieved by the unimaginable torture that the Muslims were subjected to in Mecca, the Messenger of Allah wanted to ease their suffering, even if a little, and offer them some relief. He exerted himself to the utmost to extend a helping hand to each of them and help them find relief from their suffering. Not only did he sacrifice everything that he had to this end, he also spent all of his wife Khadija's wealth for his cause.

Where he had exhausted all his resources, he asked help for his Companions, just like he had encouraged Abu Bakr to buy the tortured Muslims out of slavery. His efforts led to the emancipation of many slaves, Bilal al-Habashi first and foremost.

Where he was unable to provide material support, he supported them morally and spiritually, keeping a close eye on the Muslims being perse-

---

[8] Bukhari, 6011; Muslim, 2586; Ibn Abdullah and Ibn Muhammad, *Nadrat an-Na'im*, 7:253.

[9] For further information please see Hilal and Abdullah Kara, *Kardeşlik Zamanı*.

cuted and visiting them frequently. He would tell them that the hardship they faced would not be for nothing, that they would earn Paradise in return for all that they endured, and exhorted them to be patient.

In the name of protecting not just these Companions during this time, but all Muslims until the last day, he established an unparalleled social institution as fellowship. Thus was he to prevent the defenselessness of those Muslims who were weak in terms of social status and economic means. So that they might support one another, he joined together the hands and hearts of his Companions and rendered them brothers and sisters.

One of bonds of brotherhood he established was between Bilal al-Habashi and one of his very own paternal cousins, Ubayda ibn al-Harith. Ubayda was one of the Quraysh notables, and was well-respected among Arabs. He helped Bilal constantly, offering him every possible support and protection.[10]

TRIAL OF PATIENCE

"No one has been given a better or vaster gift than patience."[11]

Born in slavery, Bilal al-Habashi had been pushed around and tyrannized since his childhood. With his freewill taken away from him, his life was placed at the disposal of the man who bought his mother and father. His master treated him as an item of his personal property, insulting and beating him at will, and even killing him if he wanted to.

Bilal patiently endured his master's persecution for years on end and could not rejoice even when he finally attained his freedom. For oppression continued without abatement. The only differences were the reasons and persons. During enslavement, he was persecuted because he was a slave, while now, he was being subjected to insult, beatings and torture because of his belief. While Bilal and his friends now had the strength to put their persecutors into place, they had to be patient for the sake of their cause. They thus endured unbearable torture for their cause not to come to any harm, gulping down their pain and not responding to the Meccan polytheists.

---

[10] Ibn Sa'd, *Tabaqat*, 3:51.
[11] Tirmidhi, Kitab al-Birr wa as-Sila, 76.

Due to the ongoing call to Islam, the Companions mounted merely a civil and passive resistance: they did not react physically to the torture, but showed utmost forbearance. They acted with incredible dedication and self-sacrifice and did not respond to what was being done to them. Else, they could have easily taken a stand against their torturers, at the cost of their own life, and could have fought to the end. But it was not waging war but winning hearts that mattered. What took precedence for them was not acting on the basis of ego, self-interest, or impulse. This was not heroism but something that anyone could do. The test was knowing exactly when and how to act for the invitation to Islam to reach its ultimate aim. In such awareness, they chose patience. Even if their carnal selves wanted so much to take a stand against the polytheists when their persecution reached insufferable proportions, they submitted to the command of Allah and His Messenger, and always endured with patience. Muslim ibn Subayh narrates:

The Companions once said to Allah's Messenger: "O Messenger of Allah, we have increased in number. Would that you divide us into groups of ten so that we could pursue the leaders of the Quraysh by night, killing them and seizing control of the city (of Mecca)."

That the Messenger of Allah was pleased with the courageousness of his Companions could be noted in the expression on his countenance. Seeing the Messenger's smile and taking what was spoken of to heart, as though it would be done at once, Uthman exclaimed,

"They are our sons, our fathers and our brothers. How can we kill them?" He repeated these words so much that all the Companions present concluded that what was first spoken of was a bad course of action.

The smile on the face of Allah's Messenger, who was displeased with the excessive repetition of these words, disappeared, and he then got up and left. After that, the Meccans continued their torture, and we, being patient."[12]

After gaining his freedom, Bilal was not subjected to the severe torture he had been exposed to before. But, he did not escape torture and persecution altogether. He too, like all the other free men and women, was insulted and mocked at every opportunity. He was still assaulted, and still shoved around. When the Muslims were blockaded by the Mec-

---

[12] Ibn Manzur, *Mukhtasar*, 5:257.

can polytheists in a certain neighborhood, he also experienced great suffering for three long years. Together they faced hunger, thirst, loneliness, and desperation. While the crying of children, the moans of the elderly, the cries of mothers shook the heavens for many a night, their hearts were torn to pieces. But the Companions did not rise to the bait of the Meccans. They did not raise arms against or fight them. Using the most effective and appropriate weapon against them for that day, they overcame all of these ordeals with patience.

Bilal al-Habashi spent these trying years in Mecca in service to Allah's Messenger, making the most of his knowledge and spiritual luminance. But there was one affliction that he experienced for the thirty days after he was forced to leave Mecca with Allah's Messenger that not only he, but Allah's Messenger himself was never able to forget. Anas ibn Malik narrates:

"The Messenger of Allah said: 'I was made to fear as no one has been made to fear. I was subjected to such torture, such suffering that no one has been subjected to. I spent thirty days and nights when neither myself nor Bilal had anything to eat, which could be eaten by any living creature, save what Bilal could hide under his arm.'"[13]

THE SYMBOL OF BELIEF

People's personalities, lifestyles, means and resources, and living conditions are very diverse. This is a kind of richness. Their different capabilities, means and statuses are reflected in their lives and in the cause to which they devote their lives. Each of those who shoulder a cause serves in accordance with their own ability and that means. The cause and call of Islam is thus manifested in thousands of hues and culminates in every sphere. The experience and social status of individuals takes on varied forms consonant with their material and economic strength, their psychological or sociological background, their scope, and their heart. Each of them walks towards the truth dyed with the hue of the Qur'an and the Prophetic Practice.

What is fitting is not for the struggle to manifest itself in this or that way, but for it to conform to the basic rules of Islam, Allah's command-

---

[13] Tirmidhi, Sifat al-Qiyama, 34; Ibn Majah, Muqaddima, 11; Ibn Manzir, *Mukhtasar*, 2:94; Ibn al-Jawzi, *Sifat as-Safwa*, 158.

ments and prohibitions, and the Messenger's practice, and for it to be true step taken towards the goal in consideration of current conditions and the material and spiritual endowments of the people of service.

The course of struggle during the Meccan period is the finest example of this. The Messenger of Allah managed this process with unrivaled success. In his struggle, he gave everyone a different responsibility, a different task. His beloved wife Khadija was his material and spiritual support in his preparation for calling the people to Islam. Abu Bakr was constantly by his side with his social status, financial strength, his heart, body and soul. Umar and Hamza lent great support to the call with their social status, and particularly their physical strength. Companions such as Abbas and Sahl ibn Amr supported the struggle by concealing their Muslim identity, while those like Hakim ibn Hizam and Abu Talib offered their support despite not having embraced Islam.

Bilal al-Habashi's slave status did not prevent his taking part in the struggle to call the people to Islam. From the moment he became Muslim, he embraced the Divine decree to, "Read," rebuilt himself by reading and translating into action all that he read, purifying his mind and heart, and with the words of Allah and His Messenger. His heart and life were illuminated with the light of belief. When the Meccan polytheists set out to intimidate the heroes of belief, dissuade them from their cause, and force idol worship and the association of partners with Allah down their throats, he responded with the words, "One! Allah is One!" He embraced this Divine Name with an incomparable earnestness. His repeated cry of Absolute Oneness while the polytheists tortured him reverberated and was raised aloft in the heavens, being erected as a banner of spirituality on Mecca's bastions. Transcending the ages, he held a light to our day and all time to come. He became the symbol of the soaring struggle of belief against *shirk* (speculating a partner to Allah), such that he became the first name that came to mind of Muslims facing a struggle of belief. His struggle illuminated the present and future days of the oppressed and planted seeds of hope into their hearts. It gave them great spiritual support, energy, and the strength to struggle and persevere. Taking his example, they made the Divine Name *Al-Ahad* a banner of spirituality and set upon the path with great love and ardor.

Bilal al-Habashi showed us the stance of belief in the face of *shirk*, and that victory is won with a matchless patience and constancy. His struggle on the path of belief began from the moment he first entered the fold of Islam. One of the first seven people to openly declare their acceptance of Islam, he consciously challenged, from day one, the polytheists and the association of partners with Allah, taking his place at the forefront of the epic civil resistance that the Muslims mounted against the Meccan polytheists. While formerly a common slave, he in a short time became the pioneer and symbol of the resistance.

Bilal was a Companion who rendered the Prophetic Tradition, "You cannot attain perfected belief until I am more beloved to you than your father, your child, and all people"[14] his life principle, and attained the honor of being included among those lives who were dedicated to Allah and His Messenger. He loved Allah and His Messenger with every part of his being and never wavered in the face of the unbearable torment of the idolaters. In all his sincerity, he rejected *shirk*, exclaiming, "One! One! Allah is One!"

His belief and love which manifested itself thus on that day, was to become manifested, following the Emigration, in the form of devoting his whole life, and even his entire existence, to the service of Allah and His Messenger. After the construction of the Prophet's Mosque, he would settle in the Suffa, a raised platform in the Mosque inhabited by the poorer Companions, spending his days and nights on the path of service.

His Lord did not disappoint him in his sincerity, opening a great many doors whereby he could serve Allah and His Messenger in the best possible way. The most important of these was holding the office of Caller to Prayer. In this way, he had the opportunity to be with and near Allah's Messenger day and night, to serve him at all times. During this time he became honored with the great favor of Allah's Messenger, and was rewarded with fulfilling the personal services of the Messenger and his household. After this, he served in a variety of special capacities, from conducting the Messenger's transactions and wedding preparations to guarding him and receiving official delegations.

---

14   Bukhari, Iman, 8; Muslim, Iman, 69–70.

CHAPTER 3

THE MEDINAN YEARS

THE EMIGRATION

Emigration is a peace-laden longing for the world for the travelers on the path of hope whose hearts beat with the ideal of living for others. It is the acumen of being able to spurn rank and station, work and opportunity for the sake of a sacred and lofty cause, the courage to leave the land and home dearer to one than life, and the passion to set sail towards distant lands at the expense of giving up on one's personal dreams. Only those heroes running in the race of service—to breast the tape and win—can put forth such self-sacrifice. Pointing to the difficult of achieving this, the Messenger of Allah says, "Emigration is indeed a great trial for those who do not lead nomadic lives."[15]

Like all other difficult undertakings, its reward is undoubtedly great also. Allah's Messenger draws attention to this saying, "Emigration is a very difficult affair," drawing attention to its great reward and motivating the Emigrants to this end.[16]

Emigration is the passion of only those with elevated ideals. It is a service to which only those valiant souls who have made earning the good pleasure of their Lord their life's mission, who aspire to conveying the message of Islam to the remotest corners of the world, can hasten to. Only those representatives of a great cause can shoulder great responsibilities, and only hearts that beat for the peace and happiness of humanity can take ownership of them. Only those heroes of the Call who make the troubles of others their own can embark upon this path.

When these blessed souls who are able to see beyond the horizons realize the gravity of the state of humanity, they cannot remain idle. They turn to their own self and say, "If I don't burn, if you don't burn, if they don't burn, how will dark turn to light?" and thus set out without looking back and without getting caught up in petty interests. They know well that if they are late, the darkness enveloping the world will eventually come to their own doorstep, and engulf one by one the loved ones they cannot bear to part with for even a moment. When devotees fail to emigrate, they darken not only their lives in this world, but their Hereafter as well. The pages of history are replete with such examples. Nations that do not have people who are able to leave their loved ones, that do not have

---

15 Nasa'i, Bay'at, 12; *Musnad*, 2:191.
16 Bukhari, Adab, 95; Muslim, Imara, 87; Abu Dawud, Jihad, 1; Nasa'i, Bay'at, 11.

heroes, have been condemned in every age to writhe under the oppression of tyrants, and have lost their world and their Hereafter.

Emigration is to burn in the flames of separation and to become cooked in the fire of longing. Allah's Messenger leads the list of those whose heart experienced such pain. Having left Mecca for the fulfilment of his mission of calling to Islam, he stopped when he reached Hazwara, a market in Mecca, and turned to face the city. With eyes filled with sadness he gazed upon the Ka'ba and then said: "By Allah, of all Allah's earth, you are the dearest, and the most beloved to me. Had I not been forced out of you, I would never have left."[17]

For those like Bilal al-Habashi, the Meccan years passed with great struggle, excruciating torture and persecution. The Companions displayed a heroic strength and unparalleled patience at all that befell them and persevered in their cause for ten years. They continued on their way relentlessly—without weariness; tirelessly making their way towards their goal. Following the death of Khadija and Abu Talib, Mecca all but ceased being a land of invitation. The polytheists who bided their time to kill Allah's Messenger were doing everything they could to prevent him from inviting to Islam. Allah opened the way for those who struggled for His sake and commanded emigration.

But where were they to go?

Who open their doors for the Messenger of Allah upon whom all doors were shut.

Who would face even giving their lives for the call of Islam?

Which stout-heart would brave taking Allah's Messenger to his native land, when many were even afraid to be seen side-by-side with him?

Allah's help was quick to come, for He was the opener of closed doors. Divine favor began with the Messenger's meeting with the natives of Medina. Several Medinans hung on his every word and submitted to Islam. One story of guidance followed another and Islam spread rapidly in Medina. When the city became suitable for emigration, the Companions sought permission from Allah's Messenger to emigrate individually or in groups. The Muslims now had a land wherein they could freely express their belief, remember and mention their Lord without fear, and

---

[17]   Tirmidhi, Manaqib, 3925; Ibn Majah, Fadl Mecca, 3108; *Musnad*, 4:305; Ibn Hibban, *Sahih*, 3708; Hakim, *Mustadrak*, 3:8; Bayhaqi, *Dala'il an-Nubuwwa*, 2:518; Qastalani, *Mawahib al-Ladunniyya*, 1:171.

fulfil the requirements of their beliefs without assault or persecution: Medina.

No longer "Yathrib" with the advent of Islam, Medina became a luminous city.

Bilal al-Habashi, too, went to sleep and awoke each day with the deep aspiration of emigrating to Medina, and dreamed of the good days he hoped to have. He was one of those who knew best that the goal could not be achieved without the dream.

He began preparations immediately. Bilal met with those of his friends such as Ammar ibn Yasir, who were considering emigrating also. They sat down, deliberated, and decided upon emigrating, planning the best way to escape the city without the knowledge of the polytheists and without getting caught and incarcerated.

The time for their departure finally came. If someone had told him that he would one day be grieved to leave this place where he was born and raised as a slave, and where he suffered all forms of persecution, he would never have believed them. A deep sorrow overtook his heart when the time for emigration drew near. His memories in Mecca flashed before his eyes in quick succession. It pained him to leave even those streets across which he was once dragged during torture. The sadness of leaving the Messenger of Allah and his Companions in Mecca only multiplied his grief. His sole consolation was that they too would emigrate soon afterwards. The emigrating Companions took leave of Allah's Messenger and stealthily left Mecca when the time arrived. They met at the designated location outside the city and headed in the direction of Medina. After a long and arduous journey and emigrating in the wake of such Companions as Abu Salama, they joined the host of the first emigrants.[18]

Like the first group, they went to Quba. Here, they were guests in the house of Sa'd ibn Khaythama, where the unmarried men lodged, as the host himself was unmarried. They lodged here until the emigration of Allah's Messenger.

Throughout the journey, Bilal al-Habashi strove to internalize the emigration. When he reached Quba, he felt as though he had attained true freedom. Despite his manumission by Abu Bakr in Mecca, he could not escape oppression and torture and had been unable to fully realize exact-

---

[18] Ibn Abi Khaythama, *Tarikh*, 3:47.

ly what was meant by real freedom. Due to the persecution, his enslavement just continued in another form. His actions were limited even if his body and soul were free. It was forbidden for him to express his thoughts, feelings and beliefs. He threw off all subjugation and repression when he reached Quba and breathed freedom to his heart's content. With the oppression lifted, he came to understand through lived experience what freedom of religion and belief meant. From this day forth, freedom would be his sine qua non, until the day he breathed his last.

The emigration of Bilal and his friends was followed by that of other Companions. Allah's Messenger himself emigrated some time after them. Those who had tried to catch the other Companions alarmed the people living in Mecca and its surrounds in order to take hold of the Messenger of Allah. Allah did not allow the enemy such an opportunity enabled the blessed travelers to reach their destination. Allah's Messenger sojourned in Quba for a fortnight, where he met with the Medinan Muslims who had come to visit him. He spoke to them about belief and Islam, which were built on the pillars of love, respect, compassion and fellowship. Together with his Companions, he built the Mosque of Quba, referred to in the Qur'an as, *"The mosque that was founded on piety and reverence for Allah."*[19] Bilal also worked in the construction of the mosque that Allah's Messenger personally helped build, carrying stones to the head mason who oversaw the construction of its walls. When the time came, he left Quba along with Allah's Messenger and went to Medina.

BEING A MEANS OF MERCY

"One who is a means to something good has a reward equal to that of its doer."[20]

Living in the land of emigration was no easy task. Adaptation was necessary to so many things—people, places, environment, climate, air and water. The Meccan and Medinan climates differed significantly from one another. This is why the emigrants experienced great difficulty initially. Many of them suffered with fever and intense pain. One or two people unable to withstand the pain were even said to have left Islam and returned to Mecca.

---

[19] See (9:108).
[20] Muslim, Imara, 133.

As related by A'isha as-Siddiqa, after the Messenger's emigration to Medina, Abu Bakr, Amir ibn Fuhayra, and Bilal al-Habashi, among many other Companions, were overtaken by fever. Lodging together at the beginning, the Companions could not withstand Medina's climate and succumbed to fever. This was an illness as serious and relentless as to bring them face to face with death. It was as acute as to make those afflicted with it lament, writhe in agony, and break out in verse from the pain.

A'isha as-Siddiqa was grieved at the condition of the Companions and visited them frequently, to inquire after their state of health. On one such visit, she asked,

"Dear father, how are you? How are you feeling?" Abu Bakr had not even the strength to raise his head and look at his daughter. He merely responded with the following poetic verses: "Every man rises among his people in the morning, while death is no more distant than the strap of his sandal." Her father's response came as a great surprise. He was clearly experiencing a lot of pain and suffering. A'isha as-Siddiqa was overcome by overwhelming sorrow. She took a few steps in the direction of Akir ibn Fuhayra.

"O Amir ibn Fuhayra," she said. "How are you? How are you feeling?" Amir took a deep breath and was visibly racked with pain. To our mother A'isha's question, he responded with the verses:

More grievous is the fear of death, rather than death itself.

I have tasted death before actually experiencing it:

The coward's death comes upon him as he sits.

Every man resists it with all his might,

like the bull protecting its skin with his horns.

Depicting the scene before her eyes, A'isha as-Siddiqa says: "By Allah, I never expected such an answer from him! Then I went over to Bilal to inquire after him. His situation was even worse than the others. He was delirious in fever, lying down in the courtyard of the house. He lifted his head slightly when he noticed me and said, moaning with pain:

"Would that I knew whether I shall ever spend a night in the valley of Mecca with the sweet rush (*idhkhir*) and panic grass (*jalil*) around me!

Would that one day I could return to the waters of Majinna;

Would the mountains of Shama and Tafil appear to me?"[21]

---

[21] Shami, *Subul al-Huda*, 3:297; Ibn Kathir, *Sira*, 1:407.

His pain and agony increasing a little more each day, Bilal's strength was all but spent. He could stand the pain no longer.

"My Lord," he exclaimed in entreaty. Curse Shayba ibn Rabi'a, Utba ibn Rabi'a and Umayya ibn Khalaf who turned us out of our own land to this land of pestilence."[22]

A'isha as-Siddiqa continues: "What I saw pained me. So I went straight to the Messenger of Allah and related to him everything I saw and heard.

I told him that they were in a state of delirium and that they did not know what they were saying. His sadness reflected in his face, the Messenger of Allah directed his gaze to the heavens and said, "O Allah, endear Medina to us as you have endeared to us Mecca, or even more so, and bless to us its food, and remove from it its fever." Answering his supplication, Allah diverted the fever away from Medina.[23]

FELLOWSHIP ANEW

The sense of brotherhood that Bilal al-Habashi got a taste of for the first time in Mecca, he felt to his core during the construction of Quba's mosque. This was because Islam had turned those who did not even look at his face or greet him during his years of enslavement, into completely different people. Now, he was working shoulder to shoulder with them in Quba, and together, the Messenger of Allah included, they carried stones and mixed mud. They worked with great enthusiasm, in a spirit of fellowship, without differentiating between slave or master, rich or poor.

He was one of the first to observe Prayer in the mosque once it had been built. When he stood with the rest of the Companions in rows behind Allah's Messenger and began the Prayer, he understood once again just what a sublime religion was Islam. Lying prostrate in worship before Allah, side by side with Abu Bakr who manumitted him, he came to better realize the difference between enslavement and servanthood.

Allah's Messenger remained in Quba for a fortnight, setting off for Medina on a Friday morning. There, he was a guest in the house of Abu Ayyub al-Ansari. The Medinan natives opened their doors for the emigrating Companions, embracing them with open arms, and received them in their homes. Once Allah's Messenger became thoroughly acquainted

---

22 Dhahabi, *Siyar A'lam an-Nubala*, 1247.

23 Ibn Abd Rabbih, *Al-Iqd al-Farid*, 7:116; Maqrizi, *Imta al-Asma*, 11:300.

with his surroundings, he gathered the Meccan and Medinan Muslims. He affected a covenant of fellowship between the Companions. During this time, Bilal al-Habashi joined in brotherhood with Medinan Abu Ruwayha of Khatham.[24]

This was not an arbitrary brotherhood affected for just a few days, but was one beyond biological brotherhood that would last for a lifetime. Embracing his brother after the ceremony, Abu Ruwayha then took him to his home, where he accommodated Bilal until the construction of his own house. He shared everything he had, up to the last morsel of his bread. When he did not lodge in the Suffa, Bilal would go to his brother's house and be at ease during his stay there as if he were in his own home.

The Companions experienced the pinnacle of Muslim fellowship, and each and every one of them presented the shining examples of their own experience of brotherhood to the broader community of the believers. Relating one of these examples, Ibn Ishaq says:

"When Umar went to Damascus (during his caliphate), the plague of Amawas broke out and as significant numbers perished in it as to require a renewal of the state register. Making an assessment of the situation, the Caliph ordered the taking of a census of all the Muslim territories. At the time, Bilal left Medina for Damascus where he hoped to spend the rest of his life struggling in the way of Allah. When Umar oversaw the compiling of the registers in Syria, he asked Bilal about whom he wished to be grouped with. Without a moment's hesitation, Bilal responded: "Abu Ruwayha. For the Messenger of Allah established brotherhood between us and I will never leave him."

So he was granted his request that his brother Abu Ruwayha be linked with him. The register of the Abyssinians was thus linked with Khatham because of Bilal's position with them, and this arrangement continues to this day in Syria.[25]

ONGOING EDUCATION AND SERVICE

Bilal al-Habashi lived in a geographical region where the concept of knowledge and learning had been forgotten, and he made the best decision of his life when he entered the folds of the religion that began with

[24] Ibn Sa'd, *Tabaqat*, 3:233–234.
[25] Ibn Sa'd, *Tabaqat*, 3:234.

the command, "Read!" He was right and his life changed completely after that day. Bilal began his learning from the moment he first met Allah's Messenger and he continued his education despite being in a harsh environment where even two Muslims did not dare come together.

As the pressure mounted, Allah's Messenger turned the House of Arqam into a school and continued providing instruction from here. Bilal came here whenever he got the chance. He would listen to the Messenger of Allah all day long, learning and memorizing the verses that were revealed to him.

Bilal's learning gained pace after his emigration to Medina. He attended the teaching circles of Allah's Messenger in Quba, in the house of Sa'd ibn Khaythama, thereafter settling in the Suffa, what could be considered a boarding university, after the construction of the Prophet's Mosque. He soon became one of the best students of the Suffa. He lived in Suffa until his marriage just a short time before the demise of Allah's Messenger. Together with the other Companions there, he received instruction, internalizing the knowledge he acquired by deliberating upon what he had learned with his friends.

Bilal's life had changed after his manumission. He had escaped all the constraints resulting from slavery, and had the opportunity to demonstrate his talents and abilities. From this point on, he dedicated his life to the service of Allah's Messenger, not leaving his side day or night. He sacrificed his entire life for the master of all beloveds.

Meanwhile, Allah's Messenger came to know Bilal much better and was quick to recognize his superior talent and intelligence. Paying Bilal special attention, he gave him the opportunity to develop his abilities. He commended his accomplishments, and rewarded his service and success with special duties.

He appointed him the first muezzin, or Caller to Prayer of the Muslim community. On account of his service, he was given the appellation, *Sayyid al-Muezzins*, or the Master of the Callers to Prayer.

Bilal saw to his personal needs of Allah's Messenger, managing his domestic affairs, which included such responsibilities as the purchase of daily requirements from the market. Due to this role, he was given the exalted title, *Khadim ar-Rasul*, Servitor of the Messenger.

He was charged with the safekeeping and distribution of public funds from the state treasury. By virtue of this role, he was known as *Khazin al-Bayt al-Mal*, or secretary of the treasury.

Fifteen years ago, nobody so much as looked at Bilal, while now, he was a figure greatly esteemed and relied upon from the first establishment of the Muslim state and appointed to critical posts. While he was, until only recently, a slave who put his master's sheep out to pasture, he was now special attendant of the head of state, assistant to the Wonder of the Age, and the one to whom the state treasury had been entrusted.

Had this situation been unique to him, one might say that this stemmed from Bilal's personal capabilities, but this was not the case. The Messenger of Allah valued each of his Companions separately, making no distinction between free or slave, rich or poor, young or old, and would concern himself with all of them individually. He would reward them and appoint them to positions of utmost importance and cruciality. These individuals, who were but to graze herds of sheep or camels in the mountains were it not for their acceptance of Islam, after becoming Muslim became army commanders, governors, jurists, and the like. They submitted themselves to Islam with all their hearts and adhered to its commandments with great sincerity. Islam freed them from slavery and shepherding and elevated them to the position of material and spiritual masterdom in this world and in the Hereafter.

Alluding to this, the Messenger of Allah praised Bilal with the following words: "The first to don the dress of Paradise after the Prophets and martyrs will be Bilal al-Habashi and the righteous Callers to Prayer."[26]

DIFFICULT TRIAL

Long having left enslavement and persecution behind, Bilal al-Habashi reached a very special position beside the Messenger of Allah and attained the honor of being his special attendant and assistant. The task of managing the financial affairs of Allah's Messenger was also consigned to Bilal. It was precisely while he held such a position that his Lord tested him with a difficult trial. Abdullah al-Hawzani relates:

---

[26] Ibn Manzur, *Mukhtasar*, 5:260.

"I was very pleased to have encountered Bilal al-Habashi in Aleppo. I hastened to him. After greeting him, I sat down with him to engage in conversation, during which, I asked,

'Bilal, tell me, how the Messenger of Allah used to spend (in the way of Allah).' Bilal said, 'He had nothing. It was I who managed his financial affairs on his behalf since the beginning of his Prophethood until the day he passed away. Whenever a Muslim came to him and he found him to be in need, he would instruct me to see to his needs. I would go, borrow some money and buy a cloak for them. I would then clothe and feed him. One of the Meccan polytheists, bothered by this, once approached me and said: 'Bilal, I am well off, so do not borrow money from anyone. Come to me instead and I will give you what you need.'

As I was unaware of his true intentions, the man's offer pleased me. So I did as he had proposed, until one day, just as I had performed the ritual ablution and stood up to recite the call to Prayer, the same polytheist approached me with a group of merchants. As soon as he saw me, he cried out: 'You, Abyssinian!' His tone of voice made me uncomfortable. When I turned to look at him, I realized that I was not mistaken. He met me with a hostile countenance and said some harsh words, before bellowing, 'Do you realize how many days remain for the end of this month (and the deadline for the payment of your debt)?' I was stunned.

Anxiously, I replied: 'The time draws near.'

'There are only four days left,' he shot back. 'I did not give you what I did to please neither you nor your friend (i.e., the Messenger of Allah). I gave it to you (knowing full well that you could not make repayment) so that you would become my slave. I will then hold you to what you owe me, and have you tending sheep as you used to do before.'"

Bilal knew exactly what being a slave meant, for this he was until just ten fifteen years ago, and he understood very well what it meant to have his freedom taken away. He began to recollect all that he had experienced and was overtaken by great fear and trepidation. Bilal goes on narrating: "I keenly felt what anyone would in such a situation, but I could not say anything to him. I merely drew away from him as quickly as I possibly could. After I observed the Night Prayer, the Messenger of Allah returned to his family. I sought permission to enter, and he granted it. Once inside, I said: 'O Messenger of Allah, may my mother and father be your ransom! The Meccan polytheist from whom I used to borrow money said such-

and-such tom me. Neither you nor I have anything with which to repay him. He will certainly put me to shame. So permit me to go to one of those tribes who have recently embraced Islam, until Allah grants His Messenger what he might use to repay my debt.' (Otherwise, he will indeed enslave me.)'

He granted me permission. So I set out until I arrived at my house and then hung my sword, spear, sandals and shield over my shoulder. When dawn broke, I set off on my way. I began walking with quick paces without looking back, in an attempt to reach my destination as soon as I possibly could. I walked without break, all the while forcing myself to stay awake when I felt sleepy. I eventually found a suitable place to sleep. When I woke up with the first glimmer of dawn and was about to set off once more, I heard someone calling out to me: 'Bilal! The Messenger of Allah calls for you!' The Companion ran to me and informed me of the situation. Pleased that things had been sorted out, I turned back. So I went until I reached him and found four load-bearing camels at the entrance. I sought permission to enter. Smiling, the Messenger of Allah said to me, 'Rejoice, O Bilal! Allah has sent you what will settle your debt.' He then asked, 'Have you not seen the four mounts at the entrance?' I said I had. 'They are all yours along with their loads,' he said. 'Upon them are clothes and items of food, presented to me as a gift by the chief of Fadak. Take them away and repay your debt.'

I did so, happily. I then went to the mosque and found the Messenger of Allah sitting there. He was alone. I greeted him and he asked me how things went.

I replied: 'Allah has settled everything His Messenger owed and he now owes nothing.' He asked, 'Is there anything left?' When I told him that there was, he said, 'Now see if you can relieve me of them (too), for I shall not see any member of my family until you have done so.'

The impoverished usually came to me when they were in need, declare their needs, and appeal for help. I would then give whatever I had in my possession. On that day, I had two dinars left. No one came to the mosque (asking for help) that day. So Allah's Messenger spent the night in the mosque, and the following day. When no one came to me on the second day either (and I still had the two dinars in my possession), the Messenger of Allah passed the night in the mosque once more. By the end of the second day, two riders came and I took them and bought them clothing and food. After observing the Night Prayer, the Messenger of Allah called me and asked me what I did with what I had.

I said, "Allah has relieved you from it, O Messenger of Allah," to he responded by glorifying and praising Allah, fearing lest he should die while it was with him. I then followed him until he came to his wives, greeting each of them in turn and inquiring after them. He then came to his place where he was to pass the night."

Completing his words, Bilal al-Habashi said, "This is the answer of the question you asked me."[27]

MASTER OF THE CALLERS TO PRAYER

"On the Day of Judgment, Bilal rides a steed with trappings of gold resplendent with emeralds, bearing a banner. The callers to Prayer follow him under this banner until they reach Paradise."[28]

PRAYER IN CONGREGATION

In the early days, the Prescribed Prayers in Mecca used to be observed in the morning and in the afternoon. The five Daily Prayers were enjoined upon the believers in the late Meccan period, with the Ascension of Allah's Messenger. At the time, Muslims used to observe the Prayer not in congregation, but individually, because of the pressure they faced. As the time for Prayer approached, the Companions would begin to plan where and how they would observe it. As such, they would quietly slip away from the people when the time came, more often than not secretly leaving the city or taking to the wilderness to observe their Prayer. Those who were not able to do so would observe the Prayer secretly in their homes. Sometimes, one of them would be caught praying, and beaten and tortured.

The Companions, who had met all that was done to them with great patience, left all this behind after their emigration to Medina. They observed their Prayer freely and peacefully, without prohibition or per-

[27] Abu Dawud, Imara, 35; Tabarani, *Al-Mu'jam al-Kabir*, 1:340; Bayhaqi, *Shu'ab al-Iman*, 2:118; Abu Nu'aym, *Hilyat al-Awliya*, 1:149; Ibn al-Jawzi, *Sifat as-Safwa*, 22; al-Hindi, *Kanz al-Ummal*, 4:39; Haythami, *Majma az-Zawa'id*, 3:126.

[28] Al-Hindi, *Kanz al-Ummal*, 33168; Ibn Manzur, *Mukhtasar*, 5:260. Related by Bilal al-Habashi.

secution. As there were no longer any obstacles or proscriptions, Prayers were observed in congregation.

First to lead the congregational Prayer were Mus'ab ibn Umayr and As'ad ibn Zurara who came to Medina to teach Islam to its people. The Muslims who came together with Islam's rapid spread throughout the city, thought it would be more appropriate it their observed their Prayer in congregation. They sent word to the Messenger of Allah and sought his permission to do so, and began congregational Prayer once permission had been granted. One Friday morning, twelve Companions met up with Mus'ab ibn Umayr and asked him to lead the Prayer for them. Mus'ab accepted and led the first Friday Prayer. From this day forth, Prayers were observed in congregation.

Nawar bint Malik conveys her observations concerning the Prayer at the time as follows:

"As'ad ibn Zurara preached to the Muslims in Medina prior to the arrival of Allah's Messenger and led them in Prayer. As'ad ibn Zurara commissioned the construction of a mosque on land belonging to Rafi' ibn Abi Amr's sons Sahl and Suhayl, which had formerly been used to dry dates, where he would gather the people and lead them in Prayer.

Upon the Messenger's arrival in Medina, he led the Prayer here until the construction of the Prophet's Mosque. I can almost see the Messenger of Allah leading the Prayer in this mosque after his emigration."[29]

The Companions also observed the congregational Prayer after they had emigrated and sojourned in Quba. The Prayer would be led by Salim, the freed slave of Abu Hudhayfa. This was an incredible scene. The Arabs who had not even viewed slaves as human beings were now praying behind one. Such drastic change in such a short space of time could only have been possible through belief. None of the Companions edified through Islam deemed a slave leading them in Prayer as anything out of the ordinary. None of them objected. Most had memorized the verses revealed until that day. They had wanted Salim to lead the congregational Prayer purely because of the fact that he recited the Qur'an better than them.

Abdullah ibn Umar says in relation to this: "The first Emigrants came to al-Usba, a place at Quba, before the arrival of the Messenger of Allah.

---

29 Shami, *Subul al-Huda*, 3:335.

These Companions, most of whom were *qurra* (reciters of the Qur'an who had committed the whole Qur'an to memory), and including such figures as Umar, observed the Prayer in congregation. Salim, the freed slave of Abu Hudhayfa, used to lead them in Prayer. Of them, he had the most knowledge of the Qur'an."

Upon the Messenger's emigration, he led the Prayer in Quba himself. In Medina, he led the Prayer at the site belonging to Sahl and Suhayl until the construction of the Prophet's Mosque.

THE FIRST CALL TO PRAYER

In Islam's early days, the call to Prayer was not recited as it is in our day. When the time for Prayer came, the people would inform one another and then go to Prayer. Bilal al-Habashi specifically used to wander about and announce the Prayer time to the people. Whenever the Prayer was to be observed, the Messenger of Allah would instruct him to, "Call the people to Prayer." Darting off, Bilal would then make his way through the streets and marketplaces announcing and inviting people to the Prayer saying, *as-salat, as-salat* (the Prayer, the Prayer), or *as-salat aj-jami'atun* (Prayer brings the people together).[30]

When the number of Muslims grew, calling them thus to Prayer proved problematic. Many people started not being able to make the congregation and there were issues concerning attendance for the Prayer. The Messenger of Allah and his Companions began seeking ways of resolving the situation.

As Islam spread, the problem only grew and Allah's Messenger felt the need to consult his Companions on the matter.

The Messenger of Allah once asked his Companions as to how to gather the people for Prayer. Some of them said: "Let us hoist a flag at the time of Prayer; when they see it, they will inform one another." But those who thought that a flag could not be seen from anywhere said that this was not a good idea. Then some of them suggested a horn. The Messenger of Allah said: "This is a practice of the Jews." Then some of them suggested sounding a bell. The Messenger of Allah said: This is a practice of the Christians," and disliked this also. Some suggested that a fire be lit at the time of the Prayer, so that the people could come when they saw it. The Mes-

---

[30] Zarqani, *Sharh al-Mawahib*, 2:195; Tabarani, *Al-Mu'jam al-Kabir*, 1:355.

senger of Allah did not take kindly to this suggestion either, as it was a Zoroastrian practice. Nothing more suitable than a bell was suggested at the time. The Messenger of Allah, however, was not pleased with this and repeatedly raised the subject for a better solution to be found. But to no avail.

What, then, would happen?

How would they inform the people of the time for Prayer?

Allah Himself provided the answer to their questions. At a time when the matter was yet on the agenda, the Prophet's Companion Abdullah ibn Zayd rushed to the Messenger of Allah. He told Allah's Messenger that he had seen a dream and began relating it:

"O Messenger of Allah, I was between sleep and wakefulness when all of a sudden a man dressed in green, carrying a bell, came to me. I asked him, 'Would you sell me your bell?'

'What will you do with it?' he asked.

'We will call the people to Prayer,' I replied.

He said: 'Shall I not teach you something better than that? Turn to face the *qibla*, and say: *Allahu Akbar, Allahu Akbar, Allahu Akbar, Allahu Akbar*... (and he taught me the call the Prayer).

The Messenger of Allah interpreted the dream as an auspicious one: "Indeed, what you have seen is truth," he said. "Now go to Bilal and convey to him what was said to you in your dream, so that he may call to the Prayer with that, for his voice is more far-sounding."[31]

Abdullah ibn Zayd rushed to Bilal, and taught the words of the call to Prayer recited to him in his dream. The Messenger of Allah then called for Bilal, instructing him in exactly when and how to recite it, and how to begin the Prayer after it.

"O Bilal," he said. "When you recite the call to Prayer, do so deliberately and slowly, and when you recite the *iqama,* be quick. Allow enough time between your call to Prayer and *iqama* for the person eating to finish what he is eating, the person drinking to finish what he is drinking, and for one who needs time to relieve himself." To the Companions, he then said:

---

[31] Bukhari, Adhan, 1; Muslim, Salat, 1; Abu Dawud, Salat, 27–28; Ibn Majah, Adhan, 1; Nasa'i, Adhan, 1; Suhayli, *Rawda al-Unf*, 2:356; Ibn al-Athir, *Usd al-Ghaba*, 2953; Zarqani, *Sharh al-Mawahib*, 2:195.

"Do not stand for the Prayer until you see me."[32]

Bilal al-Habashi recited the first ever call to Prayer on the roof of the house of the female Companion Nawar bint Malik. Her house was very close to the house of Abu Ayyub al-Ansari. Its most important feature was its being the highest of all the houses in the neighborhood. This situation was a means of great favor for her. Bilal called the people to Prayer from the top of her house until the construction of the Prophet's Mosque. She herself relates this fine scene:

"My house was the loftiest of all the houses in the environs of the mosque and Bilal used to recite the call to Prayer from it until the completion of the Prophet's Mosque. I could easily see him from my house when he called to the Prayer.

When the Mosque of the Prophet was completed, he began reciting the call to Prayer from there. A place high up atop the Prophet's Mosque was built for Bilal, from which he would recite the call to Prayer."[33]

This was the first call to Prayer ever recited on earth. Making Allah known to human beings, the call to Prayer called them to the One Allah, by purifying them of all the idols they worshiped. It declared Prophet Muhammad, peace and blessings be upon him, the Messenger of Allah and called humanity to true deliverance.

When the Caller to Prayer proclaimed, *Allahu Akbar*, "Allah is the All-Great," he declared Allah's absolute greatness, without comparison to any other living being. Such comparison would not have crossed the minds of any who knew their Lord. For it is He Who creates all beings, has full power over everything, has absolute ownership and dominion over the whole of creation, and is He with Whom supreme authority and sovereignty rests. The existence of everything depends on Him. Not even the movement of a leaf occurs outside His Will. If all the people were to come together, they could not create a single creature that He has created.

With the statement, "Allah is the All-Great," the Caller to Prayer invited the unbelievers and polytheists to rethink their ideas and beliefs and to turn back from their error.

In saying, "Allah is the All-Great," he called the believers who forgot Allah's power, might, and greatness due to their heart's besiegement by

---

[32] Tirmidhi, Salat, 29.

[33] Abu Dawud, Salat, 33; Ibn Sa'd, *Tabaqat*, 8:420; Ibn an-Najjar, *Al-Durra at-Thamina*, 201.

satanic feeling, and who did not design their lives in accordance with His commandments, to tear the veils of heedlessness, and to freeing themselves from the clutches of Satan, the carnal self, and those subjected to satanic influence.

He repeatedly invited those who turned to their Lord to learn His greatness, reflect upon it, and to remembrance and invocation of Him.

Declaring, *Ashhadu an la ilaha illa'llah* (I bear witness that there is no deity but Allah), and proclaiming his belief for all the world to hear, he invited the unbelievers and polytheists to think one more time and to see the truth, and the believers who had become caught up in the vortex of heedlessness and had who had thus begun to deviate from belief in Divine Unity, to come to their senses, free themselves from this whirlpool, and turn to their Lord. While the believers who had turned to their Lord, he invited to delve into the sea of Divine Unity and to behold Him from the window of the Divine Name *(Al-)Ahad*: The Unique One of Absolute Oneness.

Saying, *Ashhadu anna Muhammada'r-Rasulullah* (I bear witness that Muhammad is the Messenger of Allah), he invited those who denied the Prophethood of Allah's Messenger despite the thousands of proofs to come to reason, to come to know him, and to rethink the grounds for their denial. He called the believers to reread his words and life from the window of wisdom, to look once again at every aspect of his experiences and to become acquainted with and acquaint others with him in the best possible way.

In saying, *Hayya ala's-salah* (Come to the Prayer), the Caller to Prayer called the people to the presence of their Lord. He called the human being to respond to the call of the Lord Who rendered them the most honorable of all creation, with the words:

"At Your beckoning and call, O Lord! At Your service! Here I am, to taste the honor of being a servant unto You, to feel to my core the consciousness of servanthood, and to become worthy of Your grace and favor."

When calling the people to Allah's presence, the Caller invited them to say from the innermost of their hearts and thus thank Him:

"O Lord, How great You are! You created me out of nothing, bestowed upon me countless material and immaterial bounties, created me in the finest way and as the most honorable of creation. Now, You invite to Your presence, address me personally without intermediary, and seek for me to open my heart and soul to You, to share with You my feelings, to present to You my state, and to seek help from You directly.

You offer Your love, and allow for me to love You, to render You my Beloved, and to burn with love for You.

You love me because I turn my face toward You, rely on and worship You, and You open wide all eight gates of Paradise for me."

With the proclamation, *Hayya ala'l-falah* (Come to salvation), the Caller to Prayer invited the unbelievers to deliverance from unbelief, and the believers to pull away from heedlessness and wickedness, purge themselves of evil feeling, and turn to Allah with a sincere heart.

The servant standing in the presence of their Lord, says:

"My Lord! O Allah, Who honors me with His love and Who loves me! My heart brims with Your love, having been favored with Your incomparable grace. From the moment I believed in You, I have restrained my gaze from the unlawful, have not spoken words of falsehood or untruth, and have harbored good feelings towards the people. I have striven to shun heedlessness and have endeavored to be with You. Praise be to You for the innumerable blessings You have bestowed upon me.

Endless thanks be to You for favoring us with the Prayer, which is the means for remembrance, reflection and contemplation of You, which removes the veils between us and which brings us a step closer to You."

Qadi Iyad's brilliant observations concerning the call to Prayer are as follows:

The call to Prayer is a very special statement encompassing all the facets of belief. It entails both rational as well as transmitted proofs.

The statement, "Allah is the All-Great" declares Allah's existence and His attributes of perfection, and proclaims Him to be absolutely free from any kind of defect or   imperfection.

"I bear witness that there is no deity but Allah," declares Allah as being exalted above any partner they attribute to Him and proclaims His Oneness. Declaring Allah to be absolutely exalted above having any partners is the requirement of Divine Unity, and is the foremost religious duty of the believer.

With the statement "I bear witness that Muhammad is the Messenger of Allah," the essentials of belief are complete.

"Come to the Prayer" calls to worship of Allah, while "Come to salvation" calls to deliverance. This indicates being raised to life after death and the life of the Hereafter.

Belief is consolidated with the repetition of these words during the *iqama*, and a person's turning to Allah not just in word, but also in heart, is demanded."[34]

There is no doubt that Bilal al-Habashi felt much more than all this as he recited the very first call to Prayer. Serving as the Messenger's Caller to Prayer five times a day, and, as such, calling humanity to Allah, to His Messenger, to belief in Divine Oneness and Unity, and to shunning vice and wickedness must surely have led to him experiencing feelings of an ineffable nature.

Hearing Bilal's call to Prayer resonate, Umar ran to the Messenger of Allah with great excitement: "O Messenger of Allah, By the One who sent you with the truth, I saw the same dream and these self-same words were taught to me. I was ashamed to inform you of it." Allah's Messenger replied, "All praise be to Allah," Allah's Messenger then said, praising Allah for guiding his community to what is best.[35]

While the first call to Prayer was a cause of great excitement for the Muslims, it drew the anger of the Jews.

They criticized Allah's Messenger for doing what had not been done before and attempted to sow seeds of discord, making light of the call to Prayer, presuming to speak of and treating it with contempt. Upon this, the following Qur'anic verse was revealed:

"When you recite the call to the Prayer, they take it for a mockery and sport—that is because they are a people who do not use their reason to understand" (5:58).

One of the Jews went even further. When Bilal al-Habashi was reciting the call to Prayer and said, "I bear witness that Muhammad is the Messenger of Allah," he cussed and cursed saying, "May Allah burn the one who lies."

A short while after the incident, a fire broke out in the house of Jew who had cursed thus. The servant who saw the fire ran home, but there was nothing to be done when he reached it. The house had had been

---

34 Shami, *Subul al-Huda*, 3:254.
35 Abu Dawud, Salat, 28; Ibn al-Athir, *Usd al-Ghaba*, 2953.

reduced to ask and the Jewish man who was at home at the time burned to death.[36]

Overjoyed to be the Messenger's Caller to Prayer, Bilal taught a great many people how to recite the call to Prayer and trained many muezzins. To his students, he related exactly how he recited the call to Prayer:

"First, I turn to face the *qibla*, and begin calling to the Prayer by saying, 'Allah is the All-Great, Allah is the All-Great.' When reciting, 'I bear witness that there is no deity but Allah,' I turn to the right, and turn to the left when reciting, 'I bear witness that Muhammad is the Messenger of Allah.' I then turn around, turning to face the right when I say the words, 'Come to the Prayer,' and turning to face the left in saying, 'Come to salvation.' Then I return to face the Ka'ba and say, 'Allah is the All-Great; there is no deity but Allah.' I repeat the phrases twice during the call to Prayer, while only once during the iqama."

Bilal became a completely different person with his acceptance of Islam and attained his freedom when freeing persecution and emigrating to Medina. With his appointment as the Messenger's Caller to Prayer, he attained the pinnacle of Divine grace and favor.

What was the reason for this unmatched favor?

Why had he been chosen for this sublime duty?

Why would the call to Prayer that was the mark of Islam become identified with him and why was he to come to mind at the very mention of the Call, until the end of time?

Why would he be the first to whom reference was made upon mention of the call to Islam?

Was this, as Zarqani said, a reward for being the flagbearer of belief and Divine Oneness and Unity that had become immortalized with his words, "One, One, Allah is One!" in the Meccan period? On that day, Bilal called the people, with these words, to belief, by proclaiming Allah's Oneness while suffering bitterly under torture. Now, however, free from all oppression and persecution, he was calling all humanity to Divine Unity, from atop the house of Nawar bint Malik, the Prophet's Mosque, or the Ka'ba.[37]

---

[36] Suyuti, *Al-Durr al-Manthur*, 3:100.
[37] Zarqani, *Sharh al-Mawahib*, 2:197.

He was aware of the unequaled favor bestowed upon him. Nawar bint Malik's account concerning him serves as vivid demonstration of this:

"My house was the highest of all those around the mosque and Bilal used to make a call to the Morning Prayer from the top of it. He would come there before the break of dawn and wait for daybreak. Generally, he would sit and wait in a corner in front of the house, and would sometimes lie down as he waited. When he saw the first glimmer of dawn, he would praise Allah and say:

'O Allah, I seek Your help for the Quraysh that they might establish Your religion.' He would then make the call to Prayer. I never knew him to omit these words for even a single night.[38]

After the Prayer, he would not sleep, but sit in a corner by the wall. He would wait for a long time in silence, engaged in remembrance of Allah. I once approached him and asked, 'Why are you sitting here, O Abu Abdullah?'

'I am waiting for sunrise,' he replied."[39]

He had perhaps attained such distinction due to his fine service to Allah's Messenger. Who knows, maybe his wandering from street to street throughout the city to call the people to the Prayer had pleased his Lord. Whatever the reason, being a Caller to Prayer changed Bilal al-Habashi's life completely. Henceforth, he earned the honor of being in the company of Allah's Messenger day and night, not leaving his side even for an instant. Wherever the Messenger of Allah went, he followed.

BILAL AND THE CALL TO PRAYER

While the call to Prayer rendered Bilal al-Habashi inseparable from the Messenger of Allah on the one hand, it connected him to Allah and Islam on the other. From the day he began calling to the Prayer, Bilal became one with the Call, devoted his life this cause, and became annihilated in it. His life had become inextricably linked to the call to Prayer. His story also became the story of the call to Prayer. Before dawn each night, when Divine light enveloped the firmament, he would perform the ritual ablution and call to the Morning Prayer. At its completion, he would wait for

---

[38] Abu Dawud, Salat, 33.
[39] Tabarani, *Al-Mu'jam al-Kabir*, 1:338.

Allah's Messenger to come to the mosque for the Prayer and would call on him when he was delayed.

The call to Prayer had become his life's central axis. Through this means, he established a very warm bond of affection with Allah's Messenger, and grew closer and closer to him. After once reciting the call for the Morning Prayer, he waited, but Allah's Messenger did not come out for the Prayer. When Bilal went to call on him, his wife said that he had been sleeping. Taking courage from his bond of affection with Allah's Messenger, he stood in front of the Messenger's door and twice called out:

As-salatu khayrun min'an-nawm ("Prayer is better than sleep").

Hearing Bilal's call, Allah's Messenger emerged from his quarters and looked at his Companion, smiling:

"What beautiful words, O Bilal!" he said, then instructing: "Add this to the call to Prayer."

In this way, something from Bilal himself was added to the call to Prayer which would be sounded in the skies until the end of time. Many Companions witnessed his waking the Messenger of Allah up for the Morning Prayer. One such Companion was Jabir ibn Samura. He relates what he saw: "Bilal would call the Morning Prayer, and wait until he saw the Messenger of Allah come out of his house. He would then recite the *iqama*."[40]

Harith at-Taymi relates on the authority of his father that Bilal would recite the call to Prayer and would then stand by the Messenger's door to inform him that he had called for the Prayer. Sometimes he waited for longer than at other times, after which he would call out, "Come to the Prayer, Come to salvation; the Prayer, O Messenger of Allah."[41]

Bilal would not stand idle while waiting for Allah's Messenger, but would spend his time in remembrance and mention of Allah, and in reflection on His attributes and bounties. He would repeat the Qur'anic verses he had learned from the Messenger just the day before and would engage in deep contemplation on their meaning.

My Lord! What tremendous grace!

What unique favor!

What great blessing!

---

[40] Abu Dawud, Salat, 43.
[41] Ibn Sa'd, *Tabaqat*, 3:234.

Waiting by the door of the Messenger of Allah while maintaining a permanent awareness of Allah, remembering Allah and painstakingly ornamenting his heart with His love, and living in the same space and breathing the same air as His Messenger, being one with him...

He was together with not just during times of peace, but also in war. When the time for Prayer came, Allah's Messenger would instruct Bilal to recite the call to Prayer, saying, "Relieve us, O Bilal!"

By reciting the call to Prayer during military campaigns, Bilal called Allah's Messenger and his Companions to the Divine Presence. When he finished his call, he would prepare the place where the Prayer would be observed. Abyssinian King Negus al-Asham had sent the Messenger of Allah three very beautiful staffs. Allah's Messenger had given one of these to Ali and the other to Umar. The third he had given to Bilal, to plant in the ground, in the direction of the *qibla* during the Prayer.[42] Bilal would place the staff (or stick) in the direction of the *qibla* prior to the Prayer as a barrier (demarcating the space required for worship).

During military expeditions, Bilal would constantly monitor the Prayer times and alert Allah's Messenger and the Companions when the time came. He only even slept through the Prayer time once in his life, and the Companions had to make up for this missed Prayer afterwards. Qatada relates from his father:

"One night we were traveling with the Messenger of Allah (during the expedition to Tabuk). When we grew tired, we halted for rest. As we felt sleepy, one of the people said,

'O Messenger of Allah, could you appoint someone to be on guard for the Morning Prayer?' Allah's Messenger thought the same. He said, 'I am afraid you might sleep through the time for Prayer.'

Bilal said, 'I will wake you up.'

They lay down. Bilal placed his back against the saddle of his mount and turned to face the dawn. His eyes grew heavy and he fell asleep. He did not wake from sleep until he was awoken by the heat of the sun. The Companions, too, were overtaken by sleep. The Messenger of Allah was the first to wake up and the edge of the sun had already appeared when he had done so. He said, 'O Bilal, what about what you said!' Bilal said (apologetically), 'He who seized my soul seized yours also. I have never

---

42 Dhahabi, *Siyar A'lam an-Nubala*, 1247.

had such a sleep, O Messenger of Allah.' The Messenger of Allah said, 'Allah seizes your souls when He wills and returns them to you when He wills. Bilal, get up and call the people to Prayer.'"[43]

Bilal's heart was filled with a love of service and he used to call the people to the Prayer early, so that they had enough time to get ready. Knowing this, Allah's Messenger used to instruct the rest of his Companions as follows:

"Bilal's call to Prayer should not prevent any of you from taking a meal shortly before dawn, for he makes the call to alert those among you who are asleep, and so that anyone who is praying can prepare themselves for the fast. The Fajr does not come in this manner, rather it comes in this manner, and it appears along the horizon."[44]

Bilal was officially the Messenger's first and main Caller to Prayer, and this he remained until his demise. There were three other people who recited the call to Prayer for Allah's Messenger. They were Abdullah ibn Umm Maktum, Sa'd al-Qaradh, and Abu Mahdhura. If Bilal was absent for any particular reason, Abdullah ibn Umm Maktum would make the Call, and if he was not present, Abu Mahdhura would do so. But Bilal was inseparable from the Messenger of Allah and would constantly be in close proximity. On the rare occasion that he had to leave, the aforementioned Companions would recite the call to Prayer in his place.

His being a Caller to Prayer had special meaning. As he had become identified with the call to Prayer, the symbol of Islam, he was the first to come to mind at mention of it. This situation continued unchanged for centuries. For the call to Prayer was the symbol of Islam and Bilal was the symbol of the call to Prayer. This is the reason for the Messenger's saying of him: "Bilal is the master of the Callers to Prayer."[45]

The Messenger of Allah did not allow anyone else to recite the call to Prayer when Bilal was present. Someone else made the Call only in the event of his absence. Sa'd al-Qaradh offers a personal account: "I accompanied the Messenger of Allah on a military expedition. At a point, when he was alone, I heard a group of men talking in a foreign language among

---

[43] Bukhari, Mawaqit, 35; Nasa'i, 1:298; *Musnad*, 4:81; Abu Ya'la, *Musnad*, 7373; Bayhaqi, *Dala'il an-Nubuwwa*, 5:241.

[44] Abu Dawud, 2347; Ibn Majah, 1697; Nasa'i, 2:11; *Musnad*, 1:386; Abu Ya'la, *Musnad*, 5216.

[45] Dhahabi, *Siyar A'lam an-Nubala*, 1247.

themselves. I was afraid lest harm should come to him from them. I wanted to call for help, but there was nobody else around, and I did not know where everybody was. I then thought of what I could do. I immediately climbed a date palm and began reciting the call to Prayer. At its completion, Allah's Messenger asked, 'What is this Call for, O Sa'd? Who asked you to recite the call to Prayer?' I said: 'May my mother and father be your ransom, O Messenger of Allah! I saw a group of men talking among themselves in their own language and, as there was no one else around, feared harm to come to you from them. I recited the call to Prayer to summon all the people to you.' Pleased with my actions, Allah's Messenger said, 'You did the right thing. From now on, you can recite the call to Prayer when Bilal is not with me.'"[46]

SPECIAL MOMENTS

Bilal al-Habashi experienced so many special moments concerning the call to Prayer, throughout his life. The most important of these was to climb to the top of the Ka'ba on the day of Mecca's conquest and recite his first and last call to Prayer there. This call signified a declaration of the unequalled victory of Islam and the Muslims and the fact that it was recited by a freed slave had a separate importance. An unprecedented message was being given to humanity. The Meccans read this message accurately, confronted their wrongs, and rushed to Islam. Those yet unable to free themselves from the disease of tribalism and superiority, were horrified and appalled by the scene before them.

The call to Prayer's being recited by Bilal took both the Companions and the Meccans back. Everything that had happened in Mecca and the struggle against the polytheists flashed before their eyes. Their memories came flooding back. Those who were not Muslim, however, undertook a deep self-interrogation and confronted their past. Most had realized how wrong their actions were and were filled with regret. Let us go back to the conquest of Mecca and try to understand what happened on that day:

Before entering the city for conquest, the Messenger of Allah had a herald proclaim aloud:

"Whoever takes refuge in their homes are safe. Whoever enters the house of Abu Sufyan is safe." In making such a declaration, he wanted to

---

[46] Ibn Manzur, *Mukhtasar*, 5:264.

make it clear that he did not seek to exact revenge for what happened in the past. The first thing he did when the Muslim forces entered Mecca was to go to the Ka'ba and circumambulate it. Thereafter, he addressed the people of Mecca:

"O Quraysh! Surely Allah has removed from you the pride of the Era of Ignorance and its veneration of your ancestors. All humanity is descended from Adam, and Adam was made of clay." He then read the following verse from the Qur'an:

"*O humankind! Surely We have created you from a single (pair of) male and female, and made you into tribes and families so that you may know one another (and so build mutuality and cooperative relationships, not so that you may take pride in your differences of race or social rank, or breed enmities). Surely the noblest, most honorable of you in Allah's sight is the one best in piety, righteousness, and reverence for Allah. Surely Allah is All-Knowing, All-Aware*" (49:13). Thereafter, he asked the following momentous question: "O Quraysh, what do you think of the treatment that I am to accord you?"

Knowing him very well, they said: "We expect nothing but good from you. For, you are a noble son of a noble father." Allah's Messenger did not disappoint, saying, "Go now, for you are free."[47]

The Meccans, who stopped at nothing in their hostility against and persecution of the Muslims, had only just eight years ago left them with no other option but to leave Mecca and emigrate. Like this was not enough, they formed large armies to attack them and did their very best to eradicate them. While now, all this was in the past and everything had turned on its head. The Muslim forces had conquered Mecca and the lives of its people now hung on the words to fall from the lips of Allah's Messenger.

But he was the Prophet of Mercy, and had been sent to perfect noble character and morality.

He was not charged with taking revenge, but with making known his Lord and conveying His message.

He was here not to repress the people or put them to death, but to invite them to brotherhood and fellowship.

---

[47] Suhayli, *Rawda al-Unf*, 4:171.

He was here to lay plain the truth and to call the people to hold fast to it.

This is precisely what the Prophet of Mercy did. Punishing them aside, he forgave all the evils they did and set them free. In doing this, however, he did not neglect calling the people to what was good and warning them against their greatest ills and problems.

He told them that superiority was not by lineage, rank and position, or money and riches, but was by piety and righteousness. He did not merely tell them this, but showed them in action. How?

With Bilal al-Habashi, who had become the symbol of freedom.

After circumambulating the Sacred House, the Messenger of Allah sat by one of its corners and asked those next to him about its gatekeeper.

"Where is Uthman ibn Talha," he asked.

When he failed to receive a response, he instructed Bilal to find Uthman ibn Talha and for Uthman to return with the key to the Ka'ba.

When Bilal found Uthman, he informed him that Allah's Messenger summoned him to come with the key of the Ka'ba.

The key was in the safekeeping of his mother, and retrieving it was no easy task. Nonetheless, he consented.

Bilal went back to the Messenger of Allah informed him of the situation and sat down beside him. Meanwhile, Uthman ibn Talha went to his mother.

"Mother, would you hand to me the key, for indeed the Messenger of Allah has sent for me and instructs me to take it to him."

She was perturbed by her son's words, and her worry soon turned to anger: "I seek Allah's protection for you, that you will not be the one through whom the honor of our people is trampled," she screamed. Just as he had predicted, his mother was making it very difficult.

"Dear mother, if you do not give it to me, someone else will come and surely take it from you." She placed the key in the waistband of her pants, saying, "Now that's difficult. Which man can take it from here?"

Right at that moment, the voices of Abu Bakr and Umar were heard coming from outside. Umar raised his voice, "Uthman, come out here!"

Grasping the gravity of the situation, Uthman's mother said, "Here, take it, for indeed it is better that you take it, than the Taym and Adi." Uthman ibn Talha took the key and headed straight for the Ka'ba. When he handed it over to the Messenger of Allah, his uncle Abbas, who was also present, said, "O you who are dearer to me than my mother and father! Please combine the offices of *hijaba* (custodianship of the Ka'ba) and *siqaya* (water provision for the pilgrims) in us."

The Messenger of Allah instead handed the Honored Key to Uthman ibn Talha.

"Take your key, O Uthman," he said. "Today is a day of good faith."

No matter which corner of the globe one may look or at which time throughout history, one could never find a similar scene. Far from punishing the people who wronged and persecuted both him and his Companions for years on end, the Messenger of Allah forgave what they did in the past, and what is more, conferred upon many of them spiritual distinction and honor. He did this not in the pursuit of certain interests, but solely in good faith. Only a Prophet could have displayed such magnanimity, and only a believer could have understood his actions.

Such a spiritually weighty and meaning-laden act as opening the door of the Ka'ba was being undertaken not by one of the Companions of high standing, but by Uthman ibn Talha who was not yet Muslim. While the Companions hoping to enter the Ka'ba with Allah's Messenger waited with eager enthusiasm, he took with him neither Abu Bakr, nor Umar, nor Uthman or Ali. Accompanying him was Bilal al-Habahsi, who was a slave in the very same city until just a short time ago, and the son of a slave, Usama ibn Zayd, who entered the Ka'ba amidst the curious glances of those who were present. As Allah's Messenger entered the Sacred House, on one side was Bilal and on the other, Usama, the son of his freed slave Zayd ibn Harith. Allah's Messenger closed the gate behind him.[48]

This gesture of Allah's Messenger was a scene which shocked the Meccan polytheists did not view slaves as human and which turned their value judgments upside down; it was a revolution in the name of humanity that was without equal.

Having gathered to see what Allah's Messenger would do, the polytheists just could not understand the meaning behind the slaves being given such precedence, and tried to make sense of what was happening as well as the message Allah's Messenger wanted to convey. Their curiosity was short-lived. The Messenger of Allah wanted to show the Meccans that all human beings were valuable, irrespective of their race, color and social

---

48 Suhayli, *Rawda al-Unf*, 4:171.

status, that all people were equal before the law, and that nobody had any superiority over another except by piety and righteousness.

One of the most important demonstrations of this was the call to Prayer recited by Bilal. The Meccans who heard the call were as if struck dumb with astonishment and stupefaction. They thought again about all that happened and came face to face with the reality that they were not superior to a black slave.

After going around the Ka'ba seven times, he ordered Bilal to proclaim the call to Prayer. Bilal climbed to the top of the Ka'ba and began reciting the call with his resounding voice. Reverberating throughout Mecca, this sound was not just a call to the Prayer but at the same time proclamation of the end of the struggle between truth and falsehood, and the glad tidings that truth had triumphed over falsehood.

This was the most salient demonstration of the coming to light of the Qur'anic verse, "*The truth has come, and falsehood has vanished. Surely falsehood is ever bound to vanish by its very nature*" (17:81).

This was the triumph of belief over unbelief, the victory of belief in Divine Unity over *shirk*, and the success of patience and steadfastness over rank and position, brute force and torture.

This was declaration of the collapse of slavery. Ikrima ibn Abi Jahl received the message loud and clear and suffered in his grief. From his lips came the words: "Allah was most generous to Abu al-Hakam (Abu Jahl) for he did not hear this slave say what he says."

Safwan ibn Umayya, son of Bilal's torturer Umayya ibn Khalaf, shared Ikrima's sentiments. He said, "Praise be to Allah Who removed my father (from this earth) before he saw this!" Khalid ibn Asyad was no different. He said, "Praise be to Allah Who caused the death of my father so that he could not witness the day when Bilal, the son of Umm Bilal, stands above the Ka'ba." He made no effort to hide his sense of unease.[49]

It was not only the younger Meccans who were disturbed by the call to Prayer. Abu Sufyan, Attab ibn Asid, and Harith ibn Hisham who were sitting by the Ka'ba at the time, were also noticeably discomposed. Said Nursi vividly illustrates:

"After the conquest of Mecca, Bilal al-Habashi stood on the Ka'ba's roof and called the people to Prayer (*adhan*). Several leaders of the

---

49 Waqidi, *Maghazi*, 2:737, 833.

Quraysh, namely, Abu Sufyan, Attab ibn Asid, and Harith ibn Hisham, were sitting together near the Ka'ba. Attab said: 'My father is fortunate not to witness this moment.' Harith asked contemptuously: 'Could not Muhammad find someone other than this black crow to be the muezzin?'

Abu Sufyan did not comment, saying: 'I dare say nothing, for I fear these stones of Batha (i.e., Mecca) will report everything to him.' Shortly thereafter, Allah's Messenger came to them and repeated their conversation word for word. At that very moment Attab and Harith embraced Islam.

Now, those of you who do not recognize the Prophet! Consider that two stubborn leaders of the Quraysh believed after witnessing only one miracle. Consider how far you have been ruined so that you are not convinced even after hearing hundreds of his miracles, like this one, that came through *tawatur* (unanimity of consensus)."[50]

Bilal's call affected a great many. One of these was Abu Jahl's daughter Juwayriya, who had taken to the mountains surrounding Mecca with the people at the time, out of fear. When she heard Bilal proclaiming the call to Prayer at the top of his voice, as forcibly as he possibly could, she was devastated. But when he reached the statement, "I bear witness that Muhammad is the Messenger of Allah," the truth suddenly struck her and she said: "By my life, Allah has honored you and has increased you in glory."

When Bilal said, "Come to the Prayer," she said: "We will pray, but, by Allah, our hearts will never warm to those who killed our loved ones. I know well that Islam is truth, as did my father. But he did not want the disagreement of his people or to turn away from the religion of his forefathers."[51]

A youth by the name of Abu Mahdhura was another one of those vexed by the call to Prayer Bilal recited in Mecca. Sitting with a group of other youths and observing all that was happening around him, Abu Mahdhura was angered upon hearing Bilal's calling the people to Prayer and began imitating Bilal out of his anger. Abu Mahdhura had a beautiful voice. This was cause for encouragement from his friends, who urged him to continue.

---

50 Suhayli, *Rawda al-Unf*, 4:173; Said Nursi, *The Letters*, 136–137.
51 Waqidi, *Maghazi*, 2:846; Suhayli, *Rawda al-Unf*, 4:176.

Abu Mahdhura was only around sixteen years of age at the time. He continued imitating Bilal, reciting the call to Prayer in a loud voice. The Messenger of Allah heard him and instructed his Companions to bring Abu Mahdhura to him. They did so immediately. Abu Mahdhura was frightened, supposing that he was being taken to his death. Once reaching the presence of Allah's Messenger, it did not take him long to realize he was mistaken. Patting Abu Mahdhura gently on the head and chest, Allah's Messenger reassured him. Describing his feelings on that day, Abu Mahdhura used to say: "At that point, my heart was filled with belief and certainty. From that moment on, I believed with certainty that he was a Prophet of Allah."

Allah's Messenger charged him with reciting the call to Prayer. He personally taught him how he was to recite the call and said, "Go and proclaim the call to Prayer to the people of Mecca."

Now a Companion of Allah's Messenger, Abu Mahdhura called to the Prayer at the Ka'ba until his death, after which his son continued. The duty became passed on from father to son, and his descendants have been reciting the call to Prayer In Mecca for centuries.[52]

While Allah's Messenger was still in Mecca after the conquest, he asked Abu Sufyan's wife Hind, who had only just accepted Islam, how she found Islam. She said, "O Messenger of Allah, everything is very well but for three things. Would that we were not required to put our hands on our knees while bowing during the Prayer, to cover our hair, and to hear this black slave (i.e., Bilal) crow on top of the Ka'ba."

Calmly listening to her words, Allah's Messenger then said: "There can be no Prayer without bowing (ruku'). Know that the person you say to crow on top of the Ka'ba, he is a servant most beloved to Allah. As for the head covering, with what else can one cover themselves more beautifully?"[53]

THE CALL TO PRAYER RECITED IN PARADISE

Reciting the call to Prayer had very special meaning for Bilal al-Habashi. Proclaiming that there was no deity but Allah, as well as the Prophethood of Allah's Messenger, and calling the people to remembrance and mention of Allah was for him the greatest honor. When he was given the good

---

52 Suhayli, *Rawda al-Unf*, 4:177.
53 Ibn Manzur, *Mukhtasar*, 27:190.

news that this honor would continue in the Hereafter also, he considered himself the happiest of people.

Kathir ibn Murra relates:

"The Messenger of Allah once said to his Companions, 'On the Day of Judgment, Allah will bring the camels of Salih and the Prophets sent to the Thamud camel back to life by their graves. They will go to the Place of Supreme Gathering upon them.' Mu'adh ibn Jabal said,

'O Messenger of Allah, will you then be on your camel Adba'?' He replied,

'No. Rather, Fatima will mount Abda or Qaswa. I will be on Buraq, who was given to no other Prophet or Messenger but me. Bilal will be resurrected on a camel of Paradise and will recite the call to Prayer upon it, to which all the Prophets and their communities will listen. When Bilal says, "I bear witness that there is no deity but Allah and I also bear witness that Muhammad is the Messenger of Allah," the Prophets and their communities will say, "We too bear witness."'[54]

THE DIFFICULT CALL TO PRAYER

There are many moving moments that Bilal had concerning the call to Prayer. One of these was the demise of Allah's Messenger. The Companions experienced an incredible intensity of emotion when Allah's Messenger passed away, weeping whenever and wherever there was any reminder of him. The most important of all the things reminding them of him was the Prescribed Prayer that he referred to as the light of his eye. The call to Prayer came to mind at mention of the Prayer, and Bilal came to mind at mention of the call to Prayer. Whenever he made the call, the Companions would burst into tears and weep bitterly.

Bilal went into a state of shock on the day of the Messenger's passing and he could not recite the call to Prayer for several days, until the burial of Allah's Messenger. The Muslims were grieved at not being able to hear his voice. All eyes turned to Bilal, as they beckoned him to recite the call to Prayer. Bilal was not oblivious to the situation and when the time for the Prayer came, he headed towards the place where he recited the call to Prayer. He seemed to be dragging his feet. With a last effort, he ascended to the place where he made the call and began: "Allah is the All-Great!

---

54 Shami, *Subul al-Huda*, 11:63; 12:453.

Allah is the All-Great!" It was profoundly emotional. He had difficulty reciting the call and the words stuck in his throat.

When time came for, "I bear witness that Muhammad is the Messenger of Allah," his lips seemed to lock up. In one final, desperate effort, he brought himself to say, "I bear witness that Muhammad is the Messenger of Allah," and wept copiously, the tears flowing down his face wetting his beard.

All the Companions hearing the call to Prayer were moved to tears also. Sobbing, they rushed to the Prophet's Mosque. Everybody was weeping inconsolably. Umm Salama describes the day in the following words:

"After the demise of the Messenger of Allah, we withdrew to our homes and wept incessantly for days on end. We would go to his grave and would cry without break or sleep. At dawn on the third day, we heard a sound. It was the voice of Bilal. Hearing his voice only increased our mournful weeping. All of Medina wept as one voice.

When Bilal said, 'I bear witness that Muhammad is the Messenger of Allah,' the words lodged in his throat. His crying intensified and he broke down in sobs. Hearing his sobbing, the people cried even more and ran to the grave of Allah's Messenger. The streets were teeming with people and the crowds stampeded. The calamity we faced was such that whatever was to befall us thereafter would pale in comparison, when we remembered the passing away of Allah's Messenger."[55]

Bilal al-Habashi loved the Messenger of Allah more than his own self, and after this day, he could no longer recite the call the Prayer, let alone remain in Medina. Even the thought of calling to the Prayer was enough to move him to overwhelming emotion. He believed that if he recited the call to Prayer, he would be consumed in the fire of love for Allah's Messenger and did not think that he could do this ever again. So he decided to leave Medina and never to recite the call to Prayer ever again. For this reason, he approached Abu Bakr to seek his permission.

"O Caliph of the Messenger of Allah, I heard the Messenger of Allah say, 'The most virtuous deed of a believer is to strive in the way of Allah.' This is why I want to struggle in His way until I die."

---

[55] Ibn Manzur, *Mukhtasar*, 2:402.

Bilal's wanting to leave Medina pained Abu Bakr and he was extremely saddened to hear his decision.

He said, "I ask of you to stay and not to deprive us of your company." He insisted. Misunderstanding the Caliph's persistence, Bilal said, "If you freed me for yourself, then you may keep me and I will go nowhere without your permission. But if you freed me for Allah, then leave me to work for His good pleasure and approval."

"I freed you only for Allah," Abu Bakr replied, pleading with Bilal for him to stay:

"I ask you by Allah, O Bilal! For the sake of the favor and esteem I have in your eyes, please do not leave us. For I have grown old and weak and my death is near." Abu Bakr insisted upon Bilal's remaining with him in his last days. Bilal did not want to hurt him and so he accepted, staying in Medina until Abu Bakr passed away.

Two years passed. Bilal was reduced sobbing, tears and sadness at each call to the Prayer and did not give up on his desire to leave Medina. With Abu Bakr's death, he went straight to Umar, expressing his wish to leave the city. Like Abu Bakr before him Umar too wanted Bilal to stay. But, seeing Bilal's insistence, he accepted. When time came for Bilal's departure,

Umar asked him, "Who should we appoint as the Caller to Prayer?" Bilal said, "Sa'd al-Qaradh, for indeed he recited the call to Prayer in Quba for the Messenger of Allah."

It was only reluctantly that Umar consented to Bilal's departure as he knew well his spiritual stature. Umar used to speak of him with these words: "Our master Abu Bakr has freed our (other) master Bilal."[56]

With Umar's permission, Bilal left Medina for Damascus, where he went from one front line to another, participating in many conquests. But his heart and mind were forever with Allah's Messenger. Not even of for a single moment could he forget the time he spent with him. One night, he saw the Messenger of Allah in his dream. Allah's Messenger said to him, "Why such separation, O Bilal? Is it not time that you visited me?"

Bilal awaked in horror and wept at length. When he finally calmed down, he made preparations at once, traveling to Medina specifically and

56 Bukhari, Fada'il Ashab an-Nabi 23; Tabarani, *Al-Mu'jam al-Kabir*, 1:338; Ibn Hibban, *Tarikh as-Sahaba*, 105; Baghawi, *Mu'jam as-Sahaba*, 1:261; Ibn al-Jawzi, *Sifat as-Safwa*, 24; Ibn Kathir, *Jami' al-Masanid*, 986; Ibn al-Athir, *Usd al-Ghaba*, 493.

solely to visit the grave of Allah's Messenger. Once reaching his honored resting place, he wept interminably, watering his soil with his tears. Hasan and Husayn, the Messenger's grandchildren, had also come to visit his grave. When Bilal saw them he rushed to them, and greeted them with a warm embrace. Seeing Bilal proved very emotional for the two brothers. After their initial reunion and greetings, Hasan and Husayn said, "O Bilal, we really miss your calling to Prayer from the top of the Prophet's Mosque at daybreak. Would you recite it again for us?"

How could Bilal have refused those who were beloved to he who was most beloved? Knowing that his heart would not be able to bear making the call from the roof of the Prophet's Mosque as he used to when Allah's Messenger was alive, he said quietly, "Yes, I will recite it." Bilal climbed to the top of the mosque once again and began reciting the call to Prayer:

"Allah is the All-Great! Allah is the All-Great!" His voice resounded through the streets of Medina. The Medinans hearing the call stood bewildered. This sound took them back to the past to the days of utter happiness they spent with Allah's Messenger. Even if for a brief moment, they relived those days, as though Allah's Messenger was among them. The people wept profusely and the city was deluged with tears. When Bilal proclaimed, "I bear witness that there is no deity but Allah, I bear witness that there is no deity but Allah," the people wailed as they hurled themselves out of their houses, running to the Prophet's Mosque with tears streaming down their faces.

With the words, "I bear witness that Muhammad is the Messenger of Allah, I bear witness that Muhammad is the Messenger of Allah," everyone, both man and woman, young and old, had come out. The streets of Medina overflowed with people and were awash in tears, as all its people were crying. Neither before nor after this was humanity ever to behold such a sight.[57]

When Damascus was conquered, Umar visited Syria. The Muslims greatly desired to hear Bilal's call to the Prayer and appealed to Umar to persuade Bilal to recite it for them. They knew that he could not turn Umar down. They went to see him personally and pleaded with him to tell Bilal to recite the call to Prayer for them to hear. Come time for the Prayer, Umar requested Bilal to make the call and Bilal could not refuse him. Umar's freed slave Aslam offers an account of that day: "When Bilal

---

[57] Ibn al-Athir, *Usd al-Ghaba*, 493; Zarqani, *Sharh al-Mawahib*, 5:71.

began reciting the call to Prayer, all who heard him wept. I have never seen another day where the people cried like they did on that day. Though they have never heard his voice, everyone in Damascus who heard his voice that day said, "This is the call to Prayer of Bilal al-Habashi."

SUFFA DAYS

As the very first addressee of the Divine revelation which began with the decree, "Read," Allah's Messenger was tasked with communicating, expounding, explaining, teaching, and practicing it, setting an example to the people through his own life, and building a society that had fully interiorized a consciousness of revelation. For this reason, despite the overwhelming pressure he faced in Mecca, he turned the House of Arqam into an institution of teaching and learning, in which instruction was provided in intellectual, moral, and spiritual improvement and wherein worship and morality were actualized. After his emigration to Medina, he had the Mosque of the Prophet built at the very first opportunity. Leading the people in Prayer here, he educated them with his speeches, discussion circles and sermons. He saw to such affairs of state by receiving delegations, rendering judgments, and taking military and political decisions. He designated the rear section of the Prophet's Mosque for the Suffa School.

Suffa is the name of the educational institution comprised mostly of boarding students and whose instructor was the Prophet of Allah. The Messenger of Allah would visit its students every day, take a close interest in them, and would mobilize all resources to see to address their needs.

Suffa was the peerless place of erudition which trained the Muslim community's leaders in knowledge, worship and morality, the place for the heroes of the cause and call, and its exemplary heads and administrators. Here, the Companions would learn the Qur'an and painstakingly inscribe the words of Allah and His Messenger upon their hearts. They would be overjoyed to hear such Prophetic Traditions as, "All living beings in the heavens and on earth, even the fish in the sea, seek forgiveness for the seeker of knowledge, the scholar,"[58] multiplying their desire and endeavor to learn.

Suffa was the school of the heroes brought up as exemplary generations and scattered across the Muslim world to unite the people with the Qur'an and the Sunnah.

Some of those staying at Suffa would be responsible for serving the Messenger of Allah and, as such, every space they inhabited would be a school, and every minute of their life, learning. Bilal al-Habashi was one such Companion. Charged with many duties outside being the Caller to Prayer, he would spend most of his day with Allah's Messenger and would receive deep, extensive learning at every hour of the day.

VALUES EDUCATION

From the moment Allah's Messenger was commanded to convey Allah's message and call to humanity, he began to build the community. Completely uprooting value judgments of the era of Ignorance, he planted in their place those Divinely-revealed value judgments. Burgeoning out in a short space of time, these seeds began to grow and bear fruit.

The Messenger of Allah started the process of building from those closest to him and put them through an exacting process of spiritual training. Bilal was one of those who went through such a process. By learning something new every day, he made great strides in the spiritual quest. One of the first things he learned was the consciousness of perfect reliance upon Allah. Allah's Messenger intervened in his Companions with the reactions he showed at various times, and he taught Bilal to put his trust in his Lord unconditionally and without hesitation, without thought of causes or consequences. Bilal himself relates:

"The Messenger of Allah once said to me, 'O Bilal, appear before Allah as a poor man and not as a rich man.' I asked, 'How can I do so? What must I do to achieve this, O Messenger of Allah?'

He said, 'When Allah gives to you, do not withhold it, and do not hesitate to give it away when someone in need asks it from you.'

---

[58]   Ibn Majah, Muqaddima, 20.

I asked, 'Will I be able to do this?' The Messenger of Allah said (indicating the gravity of the matter), 'You must do so, otherwise you will be of the Fire.'"[59]

Engraving the Messenger's advice on to his heart, Bilal became acquainted with a new hue of reliance in Allah with each day, through the things that he heard and experienced. Anas ibn Malik describes a related incident as follows:

Two birds were given as gifts to the Messenger of Allah. Bilal al-Habashi was tasked with receiving them. He had one of them prepared and presented it to the Messenger of Allah, putting the other aside. The following morning, Allah's Messenger asked those Companions who used to attend to his personal affairs if they had anything to eat. They prepared the second bird and presented it for him to eat. The Messenger of Allah asked, "Where did this come from?" Bilal said, "I saved it for you, O Messenger of Allah!," he said. While most people would have perhaps expected thanks, Bilal received a most surprising answer. Allah's Messenger said, "O Bilal, fear not that the Owner of the Supreme Throne will reduce your sustenance. Allah sends the sustenance for each day separately." Such was the manner in which Allah's Messenger taught Bilal, and through him all believers to come to the end of time, perfect reliance on Allah.[60]

The Messenger of Allah was particular in the matter of trust and reliance in Allah and reminded his Companions of this frequently. Abdullah ibn Mas'ud narrates:

"The Messenger of Allah once went to Bilal's house and saw a heap of dates therein. He was displeased with what he saw. He did not take kindly to hoarding food at a time and in a place when the people went to sleep satiated one night and hungry the next, whatever the reason. 'What is this?' he asked. Bilal said, 'I have stored this for you and your guests.' Continuing his instruction in complete trust in Allah, Allah's Messenger said, 'Are you not afraid that the Fire will reach you? Distribute these immediately to those who are in need, for the sake of Allah, and do not fear that Allah will withhold it from you.'"[61]

59 Tabarani, *Al-Mu'jam al-Kabir*, 1:341; Ibn Manzur, *Mukhtasar*, 5:263.
60 Ibn Manzur, *Mukhtasar*, 28:71.
61 Abu Ya'la, *Musnad*, 6014; Abu Nu'aym, *Hilyat al-Awliya*, 1:149.

BEING LIKE THE EARTH IN HUMILITY

Holding the Messenger of Allah up as an example, Bilal al-Habashi became exemplary in word and action. He would never lie, no matter what the reason, would not deceive anyone, or spoke in a roundabout way, or misleadingly. Despite being honored with the innumerable praises of Allah's Messenger, he never became arrogant. He projected elevated moral character traits, frame by frame, on to his life, in a manner that commanded attention.

Another narration is as follows:

"When the people came to Bilal and sat and conversed with him, the subject of discussion generally shifted to his virtues. The people would praise him, enumerating Allah's favors upon him. No matter what the people said, he would not become arrogant, but would humbly say every time, 'Indeed, I am merely an Abyssinian, who was until only yesterday, but a slave.' Far from pleasing him, it grieved him when some from among them exaggerated their praise to hold him to be superior to Abu Bakr. He would say, 'Do not speak such words. How can you hold me in greater esteem that he, when I am but one of his good works.'"[62]

Amr ibn Maymun relates another example:

"Bilal had a brother by the name of Khalid, who told people that he was an Arab so as to lend credibility to his person. Khalid sought to contract marriage with a woman of nobility, from a respectable Arab tribe. When the family of the bride turned him down, he told them that he brother to Bilal al-Habashi. The family's attitude changed immediately.

They said, 'If you bring Bilal with you, we will sanction the marriage.' Khalid ibn Rabah went straight to Bilal and explained the situation, requesting Bilal to intercede on his behalf."

Bilal disapproved of his brother's efforts to hide the fact that he was not an Arab, seeing this as a moral weakness. He was, therefore, reluctant to vouch for him. But he could not turn down his brother's request. So Bilal went with him to the house of the bride.

The family were very honored at Bilal's visiting their home. They met him at the door and welcomed him, showing him to the best seat in the house. When the Companions sat down, they inquired about their health, and after a short conversation, delved straight into the reason for their

---

[62] Ibn Manzur, *Mukhtasar*, 5:267.

visit. The family members present asked Bilal what kind of man his brother was. Bilal did not want to say anything unfavorable about his brother, but he did not want to mislead them either. He thus told them the truth, in the clearest possible terms:

"I am Bilal ibn Rabah and this is my brother. He is of not of perfect moral character, and it cannot be said that he observes much worship. After obtaining all the information you seek concerning him, you may give your daughter to him in marriage, or refuse. We will understand either way." Appreciating such a clear-cut testimony, the bride's family gladly accepted the proposal, and said, "We shall be pleased to give your brother our daughter's hand in marriage." The marriage ceremony and wedding were thereafter conducted.[63]

THE HERO OF COMPASSION AND MERCY

Bilal, who had been maltreated, despised and wronged his whole life, was subjected to unbelievable cruelty and persecution. His life had completely changed with his acceptance of Islam. He first escaped the oppression spiritually and then physically. Far from provoking him to anger, the torture and oppression he endured made him a hero of compassion and mercy. Whenever he saw someone who was in need of help, he felt the pain of this deep inside. He became one of those who saved his worldly life, as well his life in the Hereafter, by rushing to the aid of others, no matter what state they were in.

Bilal himself relates: "I was once walking by the house of Fatima, on my way to the Prayer, when I heard the sound of weeping. It was coming from Fatima's house. Thinking that she needed help, I sought permission and entered. When I walked in, Fatima was grinding flour while her son Husayn was near the mill, crying. Though it was time for the Prayer, I could not bear to leave them in such a state. So I asked her, "Can I be of help to you?" When she said that I could, I said, "If you wish, I can grind the flour, or I can take the child while you grind the flour."

"I can take the child," she replied.

After grinding the remaining flour, I rushed back to the Prophet's Mosque, but was late nonetheless. The call to Prayer had been recited and

---

63 Ibn Sa'd, *Tabaqat*, 3:237.

the Prayer observed. When the Messenger of Allah saw me he asked, 'Where have you been, O Bilal?'

I said, "I stopped by Fatima's house and when I saw that she was grinding flour and her son was crying, I took over the grinding and that is why I am late." Pleased with Bilal's actions, the Messenger of Allah made the following supplication: "You showed mercy to her, may Allah show mercy to you."[64]

In Mecca, Bilal saw nothing but hardheartedness, violence and persecution by his masters. It was from the Muslims that he learned compassion and mercy. He was astounded to see that the believers, each a symbol of compassion and mercy, treated even trees with mercy.

Accompanying Allah's Messenger in the conquest of Khaybar, Bilal, as always, never left the Messenger's side throughout the siege. Towards the end of the battle, the Natat fort, one of the most heavily fortified, was besieged, the Muslims faced serious resistance. The siege dragged on. One of the Companions suggested that they cut down the date palms to weaken the resistance of the Jews, as was previously utilized as a war tactic. Abu Bakr intervened before such a suggestion was implemented, and said, "O Messenger of Allah, surely Allah, the Most High, has promised you Khaybar, and He will fulfill what He has promised you. So do not cut down the date palms."

The Messenger of Allah decided against the cutting of the date palms. He commanded Bilal al-Habashi to call out to the people and prevent them from cutting the date palms.[65]

One of the pivotal events that taught Bilal to be sensitive in relation to being compassionate and merciful toward the people was again experienced during the Khaybar siege. One of the Companions came to Allah's Messenger and said of Safiyya, the daughter of Banu Nadir chief Huyayy ibn Akhtab, that were one of the Companions to wed her, this could be cause for resentment among them, and that Allah's Messenger himself should take her in marriage.

The Messenger of Allah thus sent Bilal to bring her. Bilal went straight to the fortress where they were being kept. When he arrived, he found her to be with her paternal cousin. He told them that they needed to go with him to Allah's Messenger. Bilal led them passed the slain and her

64 Ibn Manzur, *Mukhtasar*, 5:263.
65 Waqidi, *Maghazi*, 2:645.

cousin screamed, her cry resounding across the battlefield. Allah's Messenger heard Safiyya's cousin and asked what had happened. The reason distressed him. When Bilal was brought to him, he reproached him saying, "O Bilal, has all compassion left you that you lead these women past the dead!" Bilal said, apologetically, "O Messenger of Allah, I did not think that you would disapprove of my wanting her to see the destruction of her people."[66]

DEVOTEE

One of the most important lessons that Bilal learned was to serve the cause of Islam and Divine Unity, for the sake of Allah and His Messenger, and to support those upholding the cause. Bilal fulfilled this perfectly and became of the true devotees of the cause. He dedicated his entire life to service, spending his time, all his resources and capabilities in this way. He rose to the summit of self-sacrifice without rest or break, day or night. His life was filled with scenes of altruism. One such scene was experienced during the Battle of the Trench.

The Muslims suffered unimaginable difficulties and had to contend with hunger, thirst, fear, cold, storms and the enemy at one and the same time. The Companions could find nothing warm to wear in the freezing cold, facing the enemy in nothing more than a thin layer of clothing. They shivered in the biting cold, sought shelter when night fell, against the lashing wind and storms, and could not get out until morning. Bilal did not neglect his duties even during such hard times. Overcoming all difficulties, he went to the site used as a place of worship, to make the call for the Prayer. He describes what happened thereafter:

"It was an exceptionally cold day. I woke up early in the morning. When the time came, I recited the call to Prayer and began waiting. Nobody came for the Prayer, except the Messenger of Allah. He sat down and waited for the people to come. I became restless when I saw that nobody was coming or going. I went out and circled the battlefield three times to call the people to the Prayer. But there was still nobody to be seen. Seeing my agitation, the Messenger of Allah asked, "What happened? Where are all the people?"

---

[66] Ibn Hisham, *Sira*, 3–4:336; Waqidi, *Maghazi*, 2:673.

"It seems that the extreme cold has prevented them from coming to Prayer," I answered. Saddened by the state of the Companions, Allah's Messenger entreated Allah with the words,

"O Allah, remove from them the cold." It was not long before the weather relented and the people started coming to the Prayer. The cold was not a problem from that day on, and there were even times when I saw the Companions coming for the Morning Prayer trying to cool off from the heat."[67]

His competing in the race of service did not keep him from his worship. He never neglected his responsibilities, endeavoring to turn to his Lord at every opportunity and earn His good pleasure and approval. This he indeed earned. It is related from Abu Hurayra and Burayda ibn al-Husayb that the Messenger of Allah once said to Bilal after the Morning Prayer, 'Bilal, tell me that deed of righteousness you have done since entering Islam which gives you the most reason to hope, for I heard the sound of your footsteps ahead of me in Paradise.' He said, 'I have done nothing to justify any hope than that of never taking ablution at any time of the night or day without then observing Prayers after that ablution, as much as is willed for me to pray.'"[68]

His intensive service often kept him from worldly affairs and social activities. This situation would weigh down on and distress him particularly at times when he suffered economic hardship. On one such day, he went to the Messenger of Allah and said, "O Messenger of Allah, the people engage in trade, pursuing their livelihoods during the day and working in fields and orchards, and retire to their homes for rest when they are tired. But we cannot do any of this." Comforting him, Allah's Messenger said, "The Callers to Prayer will have the longest necks on the Day of Resurrection.'"[69]

---

[67] Tabarani, *Al-Mu'jam al-Kabir*, 1:351; Abu Nu'aym, *Ma'rifat as-Sahaba*, 1133; Ibn Kathir, *Jami' al-Masanid*, 951; Ibn al-Athir, *Usd al-Ghaba*, 493.

[68] Bukhari, Tahajjud, 17; Muslim, Fada'il as-Sahaba, 108; Tirmidhi, 3689; *Musnad*, 5:354; Abu Ya'la, *Musnad*, 6078; Tabarani, *Al-Mu'jam al-Kabir*, 1:337; Ibn al-Jawzi, *Sifat as-Safwa*, 24; Abu Nu'aym, *Hilyat al-Awliya*, 1:150.

[69] Ibn Majah, 725; *Musnad*, 4:95; Abu Ya'la, *Musnad*, 7347; Tabarani, *Al-Mu'jam al-Kabir*, 1:355; Ibn Manzur, *Mukhtasar*, 22:188.

THE PROPHET'S NOBLES

Reaching the heights of belief, Bilal worshipped his Lord with great sincerity, and served His Messenger without stopping. His efforts were not in vain. Favored by Allah's Messenger himself, he was heralded with being one of those distinguished personalities closest to him. Ali narrates:

"The Messenger of Allah said: 'Indeed every Prophet is given seven Nobles (select attendants)'—or he said: 'guardians'—'and I was given fourteen.' We said: 'Who are they?' He said: 'Myself, my two sons (Hasan and Husayn), Ja'far, Hamza, Abu Bakr, Umar, Mus'ab ibn Umayr, Bilal, Salman, Ammar, Miqdad, Abu Dharr, and Abdullah ibn Mas'ud.[70]

His devoting his life to Islam and the great love he had for Allah and His Messenger did not go unanswered. Allah and His Messenger loved him too, and very much. The Messenger of Allah did not hide his affection for him, openly expressing it when the occasion arose. As narrated by Ubada ibn as-Samit: "I was once next to the Messenger of Allah when there were no other Companions around him. So I asked, 'O Messenger of Allah, which of your Companions do you love more, so that we, too, can love them.'

'I will tell you, O Ubada, as long as you do not disclose my words to anyone while I am still alive. The person I love most is Abu Bakr, then Umar, then Ali, and then Uthman.' Then he remained silent.

I asked, 'Then who, O Messenger of Allah?'

He said, 'These are none other than Zubayr, Talha, Sa'd ibn Abi Waqqas, Abu Ubayda ibn al-Jarrah, Mu'adh ibn Jabal, Abu Talha, Abu Ayyub al-Ansari, you, O Ubada, Ubayy ibn Ka'b, Abu Darda, Ibn Mas'ud, and Ibn Awf, and from the freed slaves, Salman, Suhayb ibn Sinan, Bilal al-Habashi, and Ammar ibn Yasir.'

EXUDING RADIANCE

Bilal al-Habashi projected the knowledge, erudition and learning he received from the Messenger of Allah on to every facet of his life, and became an example to the people in word, action, attitude, and way of life. He related to the people all that he saw and heard from Allah's Messenger and everything he went through with him, until his last breath. Enlightening them, he united them with the Qur'an and the Prophetic Practice.

[70] Tirmidhi, Manaqib, 30.

Those who knew him and who were acquainted with the roles that he undertook, were well aware of the serious knowledge he possessed in relation to worship and trade. They would thus call on him frequently and ask him questions concerning the life and actions of Allah's Messenger. He was never bothered by this; far from it, he would relate all that he knew and enlighten the people.

The call to Prayer, the Prayer, and the times for Prayer headed the list of those topics in which he was most well versed. He was an expert on each of them. Those who knew him knew of these qualities and when they went to visit him, would ask him questions on these matters most. In response to one particular question in relation to how rows needed to be formed during congregational Prayer, Bilal said, "The Messenger of Allah would want for our shoulders to be aligned during the Prayer."[71]

Not just the people, but even the leading Companions would ask him questions and benefit from his knowledge and insight. One of them was one of the ten Companions who were promised Paradise, Abdurrahman ibn al-Awf. He once encountered Bilal on the street and asked him a question that had been preoccupying him for many weeks:

"How did the Messenger of Allah take the ritual ablution, and wipe over his the inner shoes or leather socks (khuffayn)." Bilal listened carefully to the question.

"After relieving himself, he would call for water in a vessel and wash his hands up to the wrists three times, followed by his face," he began.

Bilal then described the ablution and wiping over the inner shoes or leather socks, saying, "He would then wipe over his turban and his leather socks."[72]

Harith ibn Mu'awiya relates another example:

"Abu Jandal and I were taking ablution and talking about wiping over leather socks, instead of washing the feet, when Bilal passed by.

We asked him if he could relate what he saw and heard from Allah's Messenger on the matter of removing the leather socks and he related the Prophetic Tradition, 'Wipe over indoor shoes and thick socks.' We then asked for how long we could wipe over our leather socks without removing them.

71 Ibn Manzur, *Mukhtasar*, 23:91.
72 Tabarani, *Al-Mu'jam al-Kabir*, 1:359–360.

He said, 'The Messenger of Allah appointed three days and nights for the traveler and one day and night for the resident.' While Abu Jandal was going to take off his leather socks, he left them on after hearing these words.[73]

One of the things the Companions wanted to learn about most was the inside of the Ka'ba and what Allah's Messenger did while in there on the day of Mecca's conquest. So wishing that they had been able to share that special moment with Allah's Messenger, the Companions were most curious about what happened inside. One of these was the scholar of the community, Abdullah ibn Umar. He provides a vivid account of that unforgettable day.

Someone came to Ibn Umar and told him, 'The Messenger of Allah has just entered the Ka'ba.' Ibn Umar said, 'I arrived to find that the Messenger of Allah had already left, but I found Bilal standing between the two doors. I asked Bilal saying, 'Did the Messenger of Allah pray inside the Ka'ba?'

He said, 'Yes, he observed two units of Prayer between the two pillars on the left as you enter. Then he came out and prayed two units of Prayer facing the Ka'ba.'"[74]

While Bilal rushed from one front to another on the one hand during his time in Damascus, he used to also come together with the people on the other, to discuss matters of faith and religion. During their gatherings, he would offer guidance to his listeners, relating to them the Traditions of Allah's Messenger and the immortal moments he lived with him. He would talk about Islam in line with the Prophetic method, enlightening the people with wisdom and wise counsel.

Sulayman ibn Burayda narrates: "Bilal entered upon the Messenger of Allah as he was eating. The Messenger of Allah said to him, 'Come and eat, O Bilal.'

He said, 'I am fasting, O Messenger of Allah.'

The Messenger of Allah said, 'We are eating our provision, and Bilal's superior provision is reserved for Paradise. Do you know, O Bilal, that the

---

[73] Bayhaqi, *Dala'il an-Nubuwwa*, 6:231, 7:231.
[74] Bukhari, Salat, 30. Note: In reference to al-Fadl ibn Abbas' relating that Allah's Messenger did not pray inside the Ka'ba when Bilal said that he did, Bukhari asserts that what Bilal said is accepted by scholars and preferable to what al-Fadl said. Bukhari, Zakat, 55.

bones of the fasting person mention and glorify Allah and the angels pray for forgiveness for him so long as food is eaten in front of him?'"[75]

While Bilal deepened in knowledge due to his constant closeness to Allah's Messenger, he strongly refrained from narrating Prophetic Traditions. For this reason, he has narrated only forty-four Traditions from Allah's Messenger. Relating Traditions on his authority were such well-known Companions as Abu Bakr, Umar, Usama ibn Zayd, Ka'b ibn Ujra, Abdullah ibn Umar, Bara ibn Adhib, Tariq ibn Shihab, and scholars from the Successors including Abu Uthman an-Nahdi, al-Aswad, Abdurrahman ibn Abi Layla, Sa'id ibn al-Musayyib, Abu Bakra, Abu Idris al-Hawlani, Sunabih, and Hakam ibn Mina.[76]

The Traditions he has narrated have come down to us, transferred from generation to generation. One of these is related by Sunabih, wherein he asks Abu al-Khayr several questions in succession. The end of their discussion reads as follows:

"I asked Sanabih, 'Did you hear anything concerning the Night of Power?'

He said, 'Yes, I did. Bilal, the Caller to Prayer of Allah's Messenger informed me that it is the seventh night of the last ten days of Ramadan.'"[77]

In one of the traditions transmitted on his authority, the Messenger of Allah says, "Every good act is charity."[78] The Companion who learned the most supplications from the Messenger of Allah recited the following supplication the most: 'O Allah, forgive me my errors and sins, and excuse my mistakes."[79]

Great scholars, in addition to such Companions such as Umar, Abdullah ibn Mas'ud, and Abdullah ibn Umar, asked him questions and related Traditions from him. As related by Abdullah ibn Umar:

"The Medinans greeted and welcomed the Messenger of Allah during his emigration, when he left Quba for Medina. I asked Bilal, 'In what manner did you see the Messenger of Allah responding to them?' He said, motioning with his hand, 'In this way.'[80]

---

[75] Ibn Manzur, *Mukhtasar*, 5:261, 23:15.
[76] Ibn Abd al-Barr, *Isti'ab*, 1:180; Abu Nu'aym, *Ma'rifat as-Sahaba*, 271; Dhahabi, *Siyar A'lam an-Nubala*, 1247.
[77] Bukhari, Maghazi, 88.
[78] Ibn Kathir, *Jami al-Masanid*, 1001.
[79] Ibn Abd Rabbih, *Al-Iqd al-Farid*, 7:88; Ibn Manzur, *Mukhtasar*, 27:196.
[80] *Musnad*, 6:12; Tabarani, *Al-Mu'jam al-Kabir*, 1:342.

One of the Traditions he transmitted was about the Prayer. The Messenger of Allah said,

"Hold fast to the late Night Prayer, for it was the way of the righteous before you, a way of drawing closer to your Lord, an expiation for evil deeds, a shield against sin, and expunger of sickness from the body."[81]

Bilal possessed as deep and extensive a learning as to raise objection to as great a scholarly authority as the Companion and Caliph Umar. When Damascus and its surrounds were conquered, he objected to Umar's judgment concerning the conquered lands. Such eminent Companions as Mu'adh ibn Jabal and Zubayr ibn al-Awwam supported Bilal in his views. Bilal penned a letter to Umar, and after reminding him of the Messenger's practice following the conquest of Khaybar, he said: "You are only entitled to one-fifth of the *fa'y* revenue. The rest of it belongs to the soldiers (who fought the battle)."

Umar objected, citing evidence from the Qur'an. Bilal and his associates presented evidence to the contrary. Bilal passed away before the matter was resolved.[82]

SERVITOR OF THE MESSENGER: HERO OF SERVICE

Given the honorific title, Servitor of the Messenger, Bilal al-Habashi, attended to the personal service of Allah's Messenger from the Meccan period onwards. He was as epitomic in sincerity and dedication as he was in sagacity and talent, and this made him a hero of service. After the emigration to Medina, his sphere of service expanded a little more with each passing day. Prior to the sounding of the call to Prayer, he used to visit street by street to personally call the people to the Prayer, saying, "Prayer brings the people together." Those who heard him would rush to the Prayer. The successful completion of this task proved a means to his becoming the Messenger's official Caller to Prayer. This office brought him ever closer to the Messenger of Allah. When he began to lodge in the Suffa, upon the construction of the Prophet's Mosque, the doors of service opened wide to him. Over time, he closely attended to virtually all the affairs of Allah's Messenger. He fulfilled any given task with great care

[81] Tirmidhi, Da'awat 101; Ibn Kathir, *Jami al-Masanid*, 993.
[82] Ibn Manzur, *Mukhtasar*, 1:231–234.

and attention, and exerted himself to the utmost to duly execute all his duties.

SERVICE TO THE NOBLE HOUSEHOLD

Bilal assisted the noble household of Allah's Messenger on such important occasions as weddings and funerals, assuming critical duties in the purchase of wedding requirements and funeral services.

When Fatima's wedding was to take place, the Messenger of Allah summoned Bilal and Umm Ayman and instructed them to go to the market with Ali and assist him with the purchase of whatever was needed.[83]

But his service did not end here. Later, he performed many services at the Messenger's behest, such as preparing wedding meals and taking him to where he wanted to go. Playing an active role in the wedding of not just Fatima, but the Mothers of the Believers of Allah's Messenger also, he took part at the forefront in the race of service. It is reported that Anas ibn Malik said, "The Prophet stopped for three days between Khaybar and Medina, and consummated his marriage with Safiyya bint Huyayy. I invited the people to his wedding feast which included neither bread nor meat.

The Messenger of Allah summoned Bilal and commanded that leather sheets be spread out on which dates, cheese and butter were placed and that was the wedding feast."[84]

Bilal's was one of the devoted souls and this meant that he rushed to the service of Allah's Messenger whatever the time or place. In time, service became an integral part of his life. While Allah's Messenger rested in his home, Bilal waited at his door. When he was in the Prophet's Mosque, Bilal saw to his personal needs and protection, and he did not leave the Messenger's side during military expeditions.

Bilal was right beside Allah's Messenger on the way to the Tabuk Campaign also. The expedition was a taxing one, where the people were stifled by the heat and wearied by hunger and exhaustion. After a long journey on foot, they halted and set up camp, and the Companions retired to rest and sleep. But the Messenger of Allah did not retire, and was instead

---

[83] Shami, *Subul al-Huda*, 11:40.
[84] Bukhari, Nikah, 38.

preoccupied with service to the people. In a flutter around him, Bilal tried to do the very best he could to help him and ease his work.

Unwilling to disturb the sleep of the others, the Messenger of Allah was busy with the burial of the Companion Abdullah Dhu al-Bijadayn. Bilal was one of the few people who helped him. Abdullah Dhu al-Bijadayn approached the Messenger of Allah just as he had set out to Tabuk and said, "O Messenger of Allah, entreat Allah to grant me martyrdom." The Messenger of Allah took the Companion by the arm and said, "O Allah, forbid his blood to the unbelievers." Supposing that he had not properly put across his desire for martyrdom, he said in a low voice, "O Messenger of Allah, this is not what I meant." The Messenger of Allah said, "Indeed, it you set out to fight for the sake of Allah and are overtaken by fever and die, you will be a martyr. If you fall from your mount and break your neck, you will be a martyr then also. Do not concern yourself with which it will be." Events transpired exactly as he had said.

When they stopped at Tabuk for several days, Abdullah Dhu al-Bijadayn was taken by fever and died. Bilal ibn al-Harith provides an account of what happened thereafter:

"I attended the Messenger of Allah, and Bilal, the Caller to Prayer, held a torch of fire standing by the grave. Abu Bakr and Umar were lowering the body of Abdullah Dhu al-Bijadayn into the grave as the Messenger of Allah himself was in the grave. Allah's Messenger said, 'Bring your brother closer to me.'

So they let him down and once he had prepared the body on its side he made the supplication, "O Allah, 'I am, this night, pleased with him; be You pleased with him also.'

Abdullah ibn Mas'ud, who transmitted the same event, used to say, 'Would that I had been the man in the grave!'"[85]

HOSTING GUESTS AND DELEGATIONS

One of Bilal's duties was attending to the comforts of the guests of Allah's Messenger. He would receive envoys and delegations, concern himself

[85] Al-Hindi, *Kanz al-Ummal*, 33593, 37269; Waqidi, *Maghazi*, 3:1014; Ibn Abd al-Barr, *Isti'ab*, 3:1003; Abu Nu'aym, *Ma'rifat as-Sahaba*, 1626; Ibn Hajar, *Isaba*, 4807, 2447; Ibn al-Athir, *Usd al-Ghaba*, 2928.

with them personally, organize their accommodation and food, sometimes serve them himself, and at other times arranging for such service.

Several Companions such as Khalid ibn Sa'id ibn al-As and Thawban
were responsible for welcoming guests. When delegations came to Medina, Allah's Messenger would assess the situation and assign the Companion he saw fit to the task.[86]

On the return from Hunayn, the Messenger of Allah sent a few of his
Companions to the surrounding tribes to collect the alms tax. Aware of
the matter, the Banu Tamim prevented the Khuza'a from giving alms. The
Messenger of Allah was informed of the situation and he sent a detachment to the region. Getting wind of the advance of the Muslim forces, the
Banu Tamim fled and went into hiding. The detachment, consisting of
fifty Bedouin riders, took captive eleven men, eleven women, and thirty
youths, taking them back with them to Medina. The Banu Tamim who
learned of the capture of their relatives went into a state of panic, immediately sending a delegation to Medina. On the arrival of the delegation
comprised of ten of their leaders, the Messenger of Allah was in the house
of A'isha as-Siddiqa, Bilal was proclaiming the call to Prayer, and the
Companions were waiting for the Prayer in the mosque. When the impa-
tient members of the delegation learned of Allah's Messenger being at
home they urged his coming out instead of waiting.

"O Muhammad, come out to us," they shouted. Their rudeness disturbed Bilal and as soon as he finished reciting the call to Prayer, he went,
stood before them and said, "Calm yourselves for indeed the Messenger
of Allah will be with you shortly."

The disrespectful manner of the men had unsettled the Companions in
the mosque also. Angered by what was happening, they raised their voices. At that moment, the Messenger of Allah came out into the mosque, and
Bilal rose for Prayer and began reciting the second call for Prayer
(*iqama*). Ignoring the words of warning, delegation members were still
rushing to meet with Allah's Messenger. During Bilal's second call for
Prayer, they turned to Allah's Messenger and complained, saying, "We
have come to you without orators and poets; will you not hear them out?"

Receiving the rudeness and incivility of the men with lenience, the
Messenger of Allah smiled, and then went to lead the Prayer. After the

---

86 Maqrizi, *Imta al-Asma*, 14:308.

Prayer, he returned to his chamber and observed two more cycles of Prayer. Then he came back out to the mosque. He received the delegation.

The orators spoke and the poets recited their verses. When the Muslim poets and orators responded to theirs, their party withdrew, for they were outdone. Allah's Messenger returned the captives. He ordered Bilal to attend to them and award each of them twelve *awqiyas* of gold (one of which is forty *dirhams*[87]). Bilal gathered all of them and distributed to them their prizes.[88]

From the end of the sixth year of emigration, the Messenger of Allah sent envoys to various kings, chieftains and religious leaders. Many delegations came to Medina after this event, and especially after the conquest of Mecca. Bilal was given the task of waiting on the delegations and seeing to their needs. He fulfilled his mission perfectly, considering everything—to the finest detail—that needed to be done to ensure the comfort of his guests, and doing his utmost to make certain that those who came left Medina satisfied. A member of the Banu Thalaba said: "When the Messenger of Allah came from Ji'rana in the eighth year of the emigration, we called upon him (in Medina) with a delegation of fourteen members. Upon our arrival, we were lodged in the house of Ramla bint Harith. Bilal al-Habashi came to the house not long after. After greeting us and inquiring after our health, he asked if there were more of us. After receiving the required information, he left, and it was not long before he returned with bread broth, milk, and butter. We ate the food and drank the milk and went for the noon Prayer when the time came. We met the Messenger of Allah on the way and said, after greeting him, 'O Messenger of Allah, we are the representatives of those of our people we have left behind us. They and we believe in Islam.'

The Messenger of Allah ordered for us to be shown hospitality and we stayed in Medina for several days. We were taught the Qur'an and the Prophetic Practice. The Messenger of Allah concerned himself with us throughout our entire stay, frequently sending Bilal with meals. When we decided to return we waited on him to bid him farewell and take leave to depart. Thereupon the Messenger of Allah said to Bilal, 'Reward them as you do to other delegates.' He brought a jar filled with pieces of gold and paid to every one of us five *uqiyyas* of it. This was too much for us, but less

---

[87] 1 *dirham* is approximately 3 grams.
[88] Waqidi, *Maghazi*, 3:976.

than what had been given to previous delegations. Bilal said, 'Please excuse me, for this is all the money I have to offer you.' We said, 'Please do not worry yourself so; this is more than enough,' and then set off on our way."[89]

Bilal would attend to the envoys of kings, chiefs and governors, and organize their service also. In line with the Messenger's orders, he would receive them in the best possible way, without failing in service and honor, to ensure that they left Medina well pleased.

It was in the month of Ramadan of the ninth year after the emigration, when the Messenger of Allah had only just returned from Tabuk. The chiefs of Himyar, Harith and Nu'aym, summoned Malik ibn Murra, who had won their trust, and sent him to Medina with a letter announcing their embracing Islam. Upon the envoy's arrival, he received an audience with Allah's Messenger where he presented to him the letter and conveyed the chiefs' message. The Messenger of Allah ordered Bilal to lodge them, honor them and feast them.

It was also Bilal who hosted delegations coming from Jerusalem, who were given audience by Allah's Messenger. When Yuhanna ibn Ru'bah, the chief of Aylah, humbled himself and lowered his head before the Messenger of Allah, Allah's Messenger intervened, signaling him to raise his head, and making peace with him the same day. The Messenger of Allah clothed him in a cloak from Yemen as a token of his contentment. A treaty was concluded at the end of the meeting, and Allah's Messenger ordered a place for him and the rest of the delegation with Bilal.[90]

INFORMING THE PUBLIC

As was the case during military expeditions, the task of informing the people and making announcements was generally undertaken by Bilal, whereby he would publicly declare the Messenger's commands. When the Messenger of Allah wanted to inform his Companions on a certain matter or when he felt the need to call upon them, he out Bilal to the task. Abdullah ibn Amr ibn al-As relates one such incident:

"When war spoils were obtained, the Messenger of Allah ordered Bilal to make a public announcement (so that everything gained in spoils could be collected). Bilal would circulate among the soldiers and make the

[89] Shami, *Subul al-Huda*, 6:295; Maqrizi, *Imta al-Asma*, 14:311.
[90] Maqrizi, *Imta al-Asma*, 2:66; Waqidi, *Maghazi*, 3:1031.

announcement three times. The people then used to come with their spoils. The Messenger of Allah would take a fifth and divide the rest."[91]

Another event is described as follows:

It was mentioned to the Messenger of Allah that a man fought fiercely in the Battle of Hunayn until he was critically wounded, and the Companions spoke of him with praise. The Messenger of Allah said, "He is among the people of the Fire." Startled by this, they merely said, "Allah and His Messenger know best." Following the man very closely, the Companions tried to ascertain the wisdom behind the Messenger's words. The man writhed in pain and when the wound worsened and his pain increased, he could no longer stand the pain of his injuries, and so he took an arrowhead from his quiver and killed himself. The Messenger of Allah commanded Bilal to proclaim, "Only the believers will enter Paradise. Allah affirms His Religion even through the dissolute."[92]

Accompanying the Messenger of Allah on the Farewell Pilgrimage, Bilal took an active role here also. On the night before the pilgrims gathered at the plain of Arafat, the Messenger of Allah wished to address his Companions and instructed Bilal to call out to the people for them to be silent. Bilal walked among the pilgrims, announcing that Allah's Messenger was to address them and that they needed to remain silent and listen.

The pilgrims who heard him waited in silence and Allah's Messenger spoke to them of the merit of entreating Allah in supplication at Arafat.[93]

The Muslims, who had gone to Mecca for the minor pilgrimage on the year the Treaty of Hudaybiya was concluded, returned when they were not admitted into the city. The pilgrimage had been postponed as per terms of the treaty. The Muslims turned back in sorrow, but agreed upon returning the following year for a compensatory pilgrimage. In accordance with the terms of the pact, they had to leave Mecca immediately after their pilgrimage. When the time for departure came, the Messenger of Allah instructed Bilal to make an announcement to the pilgrims that they needed to leave the city before nightfall, and that the sun should not set upon any of them in Mecca. Bilal made the call, walking among the Companions and repeating the Messenger's command.[94]

---

[91] Abu Dawud, Jihad, 134; Shami, *Subul al-Huda*, 10:489.

[92] Waqidi, *Maghazi*, 3:915.

[93] Ibn Manzur, *Mukhtasar*, 18:291.

[94] Ibn Manzur, *Mukhtasar*, 7:291.

STEWARDSHIP AND PROTECTION

The roles of steward and guardian were among Bilal al-Habashi's most important roles. Bilal would guard the Messenger of Allah even during his sermons, and would alternate with the other Companions as chief steward of the noble household. It is related that Zaynab, the wife of Abdullah (ibn Mas'ud), said, "I was in the mosque and heard the Messenger of Allah say, 'Give in charity, even if it be of your jewelry.' I went straight to Abdullah and said, 'You are a man of little wealth, and the Messenger of Allah has commanded us to give in charity, so go and ask the Messenger of Allah whether it is permissible for me to give my charity to you. Otherwise, I shall give it to someone else.' He said, 'You had better go and ask.' So I went and saw another woman of the Helpers at the door of the Messenger of Allah who also had the same question. The Messenger of Allah had withdrawn for rest (so we did not wish to disturb him). Bilal passed by us and we said to him, 'Would you ask the Messenger of Allah whether women can give charity to their husbands and the orphans in their care? But do not tell him who we are.' He went in and asked the Messenger of Allah (what the women had instructed him to ask).

The Messenger of Allah asked, 'Who are they?'

Bilal said, 'One of the women of the Helpers, and Zaynab.'

The Messenger of Allah asked, 'Which Zaynab?'

Bilal said, 'The wife of Abdullah.'

The Messenger of Allah called us in. When we went in, I asked, 'O Messenger of Allah, today you commanded us to give for the sake of Allah. I have some jewelry, which I would like to give in charity. My husband and my children are much in need of it. Can I give the charity to them?' The Messenger of Allah said, 'He said, "Yes, and for you there are two rewards: the reward for maintaining the ties of kinship, and the reward for giving charity."'

VARIOUS STATE SERVICES

Bilal was not merely charged with making announcements, but was responsible for all matters relating to public service, especially economic affairs. Abdullah ibn Abi Awfa describes one of these:

"I was sitting with the Messenger of Allah when an orphan came and said, 'O Messenger of Allah, I am an orphan whose mother was widowed.

I have sisters at home and we have nothing left to eat. Could you give to us from the provisions that Allah has bestowed upon you?' He then said, 'May Allah bestow upon you until you are well pleased.'

The Messenger of Allah said to the child, 'What beautiful words you have spoken.' He then summoned Bilal, instructing him to take the child to his wives for them to give the child whatever they had at home. Bilal took the child with him and went.

There was nothing except twenty-one dates in the homes of his wives and they gave everything they had to Bilal. Bilal took the dates and went straight to Allah's Messenger. Bilal placed the dates in his hand, and the Messenger of Allah raised his hands aloft and entreated Allah for their increase. He then gave the child the dates and said, 'Seven of these are for you, seven for your mother, and seven for your sisters. Eat one in the morning and at night.' The child then left the Prophet's Mosque. Looking on and moved by what he saw, Mu'adh ibn Jabal rushed to the orphan, put his hand on his shoulder, and stroked his head.

He then made the supplication, 'May Allah save orphans from being in need of others, and may He send you someone who can take the place of your father.' He then saw the child off. Mu'adh ibn Jabal's actions pleased Allah's Messenger exceedingly. The Messenger of Allah said to him, 'I saw what you did, O Mu'adh! What was it that made you do what you did?'

'My compassion, O Messenger of Allah,' Mu'adh replied. The Messenger of Allah then said, 'I swear by Him in Whose Hand is Muhammad's soul, whoever assumes guardianship of an orphan, and does this beautifully, without injuring or offending them, and places their hand on their head (in kindness), Allah the Most High will raise them by ten degrees for every strand of hair on the head of that orphan, record for them ten good deeds, and erase ten of their sins for each and every strand over which their hand passes.'"[95]

SERVICE IN MILITARY CAMPAIGNS

While Bilal was in the Suffa during peacetime, dedicating himself to knowledge, learning and service, when permission to fight was given, he joined the Muslim forces and went from military campaign to campaign with the Messenger of Allah. He faced those oppressors who perpetrated

95 Bayhaqi, *Shu'ab al-Iman*, 11042; Abu Nu'aym, *Ma'rifat as-Sahaba*, 1576.

every imaginable evil to remove Islam from the face of the earth. He fought heroically against oppression, persecution and injustice, and never left the Messenger's side on the battlefront. He made history at Badr, Uhud, Khandaq, and in all the other military campaigns, alongside the other Companions. While people fled at the most critical stages of battle, Bilal persevered and took his place among those beside and protecting Allah's Messenger.

The Meccan polytheists, who had for years turned their lives into a living hell with their torture and persecution, were still full of hate and enmity. They were acting like they were not the ones who had perpetrated such persecution and like it was not them to drove people from their homelands. They waited for any opportunity to destroy the Muslims, making use of the smallest excuse. This is why they confronted the Muslims at Badr. Just as they outnumbered them three times, they were far superior in terms of weapons. In spite of this, they rued the day they came to Badr. Seventy polytheists, Abu Jahl among them, were killed in the battle. Just as many people were taken captive.

When Bilal confronted the Meccan polytheists in the battle, the hell they put him through in Mecca flashed before his eyes. The fact that they still wanted to destroy the Muslims, even after all the torture and oppression they subjected them to, and formed armies and came all the way across the desert to face them at Badr, astounded him.

But the conditions were now very different. The period of civil resistance for the Muslims had ended, and fighting had now been allowed. Now was the time for the Bilals of the era to put their lives forth to put an end, forever, to oppression, persecution, and unbelief. It was the time to fight heroically against those who had come to force them to abandon their religion, and enslave them once more, and to demonstrate their unwavering belief in their cause. This is why they fought in a heroic manner against those who did not allow them the right to life. Bilal wounded many of the polytheists he came up against, and killed Zayd ibn Mulays who lunged at him in bitter hostility and at full force.[96]

Despite being three times in number, the Meccan polytheists could not hold their ground before the Muslims and fled. Seventy of them were taken prisoner. Among them were many leading Meccans, who, in an utter state of shock, tried to make sense of what had happened, and

---

[96] Waqidi, *Maghazi*, 1:149.

looked continuously around them, seeking a familiar face to save them from the humiliation they faced. Umayya ibn Khalaf was one of them. The tyrant who had subjected Bilal and those like him to unspeakable persecution purely because they had become Muslim, who took them to the desert and lay them across the san-baked sands to torture them, and who then stood by to taunt and deride them, had been captured, along with his son. As though having completely forgotten the unimaginable torture he put the Muslims though in Mecca until only recently, he looked for a familiar face that would save him from captivity and even death.

The battle was over, and the Muslims had begun making preparations for their return to Medina. Umayya ibn Khalaf frantically sought a way out of his predicament and rejoiced at the sight of Abdurrahman ibn al-Awf who he knew well from Mecca. Holding his son's hand, he ran to Abdurrahman and pleaded with the Prophet's Companion to save them. The Companion was at a loss as to what to do. On the one hand, he tried to help Umayya for the sake of their long-standing friendship; on the other, he remembered all that Umayya had done in Mecca, especially to Bilal, and feared making a mistake and causing the death of his friend. He himself describes what he went through at the time:

"Umayya ibn Khalaf was a friend of mine in Mecca. My (original) name was Abd Amr, but I was called Abdurrahman when I became a Muslim. This is the name I insisted people call me by thereafter, and I would not respond to those who called out to me by my former name. But most of the Meccan polytheists would insist upon using my old name, one of whom was Umayya. When we used to meet in Mecca he would call out to me saying, Abd Amr,' so I would not reply.

Then he would say, 'O Abd Amr, do you dislike the name your father gave you?' I would reply, 'Yes,' and he would say, 'As for me, I do not and will not recognize ar-Rahman, so find some name that I can call you by when we meet. You do not reply to your old name, and I will not call you by one I do not recognize.'

So, after that, he used to call me Abdullah, and I would answer him. We met and spoke many times before Badr. I tried to persuade him to accept Islam, but he refused.

On the day of Badr, after the people left, I began collecting armor on the battlefield when all of a sudden; I passed Umayya ibn Khalaf standing with his son Ali, holding him by the hand. When he saw me, he called out to me, saying, 'O Abd Amr," but I refused to reply. This time he called out, 'O Abdullah,' and I responded. Then he said, 'Are you in need of those? Are we not of more use to you than those coats of mail you carry? Leave them and take us prisoner instead.'

'By Allah, I will,' I said. So I threw aside the coats of mail and took him and his son by the hand, saying, 'Come here then,' and I took his hand and his son Ali's hand. Then I left, taking the two of them with me. Umayya said, 'I have never seen a day like this,' and then began to relate all the reasons for his astonishment.

As he spoke, I got lost in thought, asking myself whether I was doing the right thing. When I recalled the excruciating torture he put Bilal through, I began to doubt the correctness of my actions. I thought of Bilal and what he would feel if he saw me between them, holding them by the hands. It was not long before my worst fears were realized. By Allah, as I was leading them, Bilal, who was busy making dough at the time, saw him with me. He left the dough, vigorously scrubbing the dough off his hands, while running towards us.

Bilal recognized Umayya straight away. He had a painful and sudden flashback. There he was in the desert, where he was subjected to unbearable torture. There was Umayya, bringing him out under the scorching heat of the sun, making him lie on his back, and putting a huge boulder on his chest, telling him that he could stay there until he gave up the religion of Muhammad, and laughing at and making fun of him. He felt his hair stand on end, and he could not contain his anger. He called out with all his might, 'The arch-unbeliever Umayya ibn Khalaf! May I not live if he lives.'"

The narrator continues: "I said, 'Would you harm my prisoners?'

'The arch-unbeliever Umayya ibn Khalaf! May I not live if he lives,' he cried. 'Do you hear what I am saying, son of a black woman!' I screamed in panic. But he kept crying out these words in spite of my remonstrance, shouting at the top of his voice, 'O people of the Helpers, the arch-unbeliever Umayya ibn Khalaf! May I not live if he lives.'"

Abdurrahman ibn al-Awf did not look as though he would surrender him too readily.

Bilal thus continued calling out to the Medinan Muslims. The verse concerning captives had not yet been revealed, so the judgment to be given about them was not yet known. The people flocked to where Umayya was. They formed a ring round him as Abdurrahman ibn al-Awf was trying to protect him. Ignoring the words of Abdurrahman ibn al-Awf, they set upon him and killed him there and then.[97]

THE EXPEDITION OF GHATAFAN

Another one of the military expeditions in which Bilal participated was the Ghatafan expedition, some time after the Battle of Badr, in the third year after the emigration. When news of the Banu Thalaba of Ghatafan's having rallied for a raid against Medina reached Allah's Messenger, he immediately began to make preparations. The Messenger of Allah went out with a force of four hundred and fifty men and their horses. Bilal was among them and right beside Allah's Messenger. When the army approached the region, they encountered a man among them called Jabbar, from the Banu Thalaba.

The Companions asked him, "Where are you going?"

He replied, "Yathrib (Medina)."

The Companions said, "What is your purpose in Yathrib?"

He replied, "I wish to buy myself something to wear."

The Companions asked, "Have you encountered forces along the way, or have you received any news from your people?"

He said, "No, but it has reached me that Du'thur ibn al-Harith has gathered some men from his people and has left."

The Companions took him to the Messenger of Allah, and he invited him to accept Islam. Jabbar became a Muslim. He then said, "O Messenger of Allah, surely they could never face you. When they hear about your advance, they will flee to hide in the mountaintops. Allow me to come with you and lead you to their points of hiding." So the Messenger of Allah went with him and assigned him to Bilal. Bilal did not leave his side throughout the whole journey. The advancing army alighted at Dhu Amarr, where they set up camp. It then began raining intensely. They received so much rain that the Messenger of Allah and his Companions got wet, their clothes soaked through. When the rain subsided, Allah's Messenger moved away from the encampment, where he took off his clothes and hung them out to dry on a tree. He then lay down under it. One of those who had banded to attack Medina watched all that the Muslims were doing the Messenger of Allah all alone under the tree. He went

---

straight to their chief Du'thur ibn al-Harith and said, "Here's your chance! Muhammad has withdrawn from his Companions on his own, and is resting beneath a tree. We must hurry! We need not to worry about his Companions for we would have long killed him and fled before they are able to come to his aid."

Du'thur wasted no time and decided to handle the task himself to ensure that it was done properly. He chose a sword for himself, and stealthily descended from the mountain. He approached until he stood at the head of Allah's Messenger with the sword in his hand, and said, his sword drawn, "O Muhammad, now who will protect you from me?"

Allah's Messenger was neither afraid, nor even taken by surprise. He turned rather calmly to the man and said, "Allah."

Gabriel, who was right beside Allah's Messenger at that moment, pushed Du'thur in the chest, and the sword of Du'thur, who was shaken by the blow, fell from his hand. Allah's Messenger took the sword, and he stood with the sword at Du'thur's head and said, "Now, tell me, who will save you from me!" He then invited Du'thur to Islam. But Du'thur did not accept, despite the extent to which he was affected by his experience. Describing the event, Abu Burda continues: "I was nearest to the Messenger of Allah at that time. When he called out to me, I rushed to him. When I realized what had happened, I wanted to kill the man, but the Messenger of Allah did not permit me.

He said, 'Fret not, O Abu Burda, for Allah will protect me until He makes His Religion prevail over all other religions,' and then commanded me to release him. Du'thur then said, before leaving, 'By Allah, I shall never gather a force against you.'" Some narrations indicate that he accepted the Messenger's offer, and embraced Islam.

Bilal was also involved in ceremonial services, such as handing over the standard to commanders on behalf of the Messenger. When he accompanied Allah's Messenger on military expedition, he would be responsible for the Messenger's saddlery, and would serve as his steward and adjutant.

On the sixth year of the emigration, the Messenger of Allah ordered Abdurrahman ibn al-Awf to set out on expedition to Dumat al-Jandal with a group of Companions. Abdurrahman ibn al-Awf had worn a black turban of cotton. When he came to take leave of Allah's Messenger, Allah's Messenger told him to approach, and seated Abdurrahman ibn al-Awf beside him. He then unwound the turban, which he had noticed to have been wrapped in haste, and rewound it in a neater fashion, leaving four fingers or so hanging down between his shoulders. He then ordered Bilal to give Abdurrahman ibn al-Awf the standard, and he did so. Then he praised Allah, invoked salutations upon himself, and said, "Take the standard, O Ibn Awf," and relayed to him his commands and counsel for the expedition. The commander thus set off with the standard brought to him by Bilal.[98]

Bilal undertook all his services with a great love and sense of fulfilment. Even at times when he fell exhausted from fatigue, he would not lose his fervor and zeal for service, instead experiencing these to the utmost. He would never give way to the desires coming from his carnal self, and did not even dream of slackening in his service, in any way or means. Abdurrahman al-Fihri narrates:

"I was present with the Messenger of Allah at the battle of Hunayn. We travelled on a hot summer day when the heat was extreme. After a long walk, we halted under the shade of some acacia trees. When the sun passed the meridian, I put on my coat of mail and mounted my horse. I then went over to the Messenger of Allah, who was in his tent.

I said, 'Peace be upon you, O Messenger of Allah, and may His mercy and blessing be upon you. The time for our departure has come.'

'Yes, it has,' he replied. He then said, 'Rise, O Bilal.'

Bilal jumped out from beneath an acacia, where he had been curled up, his shadow like that of a bird.

He said, 'O you who are dearer to me than my mother and father! I am at your service!' The Messenger of Allah instructed, 'Saddle up my horse.' Bilal went swiftly to the horse. He then brought a saddle, both sides of which were made of palm leaves that were without holes or perforations. Bilal informed the Messenger of Allah when it was ready. The Messenger of Allah mounted his horse. He rode and so did we.

Umm Husayn was another witness of Bilal's service on military expeditions. She says:

"I performed the Farewell Pilgrimage in the company of the Messenger of Allah. I saw Usama and Bilal, one of them holding the halter of his camel, with the other raising his garment (over his head) and sheltering

98 Ibn Hisham, *Sira*, 3–4:632; Ibn Manzur, *Mukhtasar*, 14:350.

him from the sun, until he threw pebbles at the great stone pillar (*Jamrat al-Aqaba*)."[99]

Bilal would not be content just to serve Allah's Messenger in the best possible way, but held himself responsible for his safety and security, guarding him when necessary. Al-Harith al-Bakri describes a notable example as follows:

"I went to Medina to make a complaint about al-Ala al-Hadrami to the Messenger of Allah. As I passed by al-Rabdha, I came across an old woman of the Banu Tamim who had been stranded. She asked, 'O servant of Allah, I need to see the Messenger of Allah. Will you take me to him?'

So I took her along with me to Medina. We arrived to find the mosque inundated with people. A black banner was raised high, and Bilal was there girding his sword, standing in front of the Messenger of Allah."

Accompanying the Messenger of Allah in the Battle of Uhud also, Bilal persevered throughout and did not leave the Prophet's side. Allah's Messenger took several blows to his face, head and shoulder during the conflict. After the battle, it was almost evening when he returned to Medina. Allah's Messenger could barely stand from the pain of the wounds he sustained, and was only able to enter his house leaning on Sa'd ibn Ubada and Sa'd ibn Mu'adh. Hearing Bilal pronounce the call to Prayer after the sun set the Messenger of Allah came out, as he went in, leaning on the two Sa'ds. He returned to his house afterwards in the same manner. As he rested in his house, the people in the mosque lit fires and cauterized the wounds.

Then Bilal called for the Night Prayer for when the time came. However, the Messenger of Allah could not come out from his exhaustion. Bilal was also extremely weary, but no matter what his condition was, he could not rest, nor sleep while Allah's Messenger was in such a state. Bilal waited at his door until a third of the night had passed. Prominent Medinans did not go to their homes that night either, waiting in front of the Messenger's door in case of a raid. Toward morning, Bilal called out to him, saying, "The Prayer, O Messenger of Allah." The Messenger of Allah came out, and it was clear that he had been sleeping. The sleep appeared to have helped, for he seemed a little better. He made ablution and observed the Prayer, and was able to return to his house unaided. Bilal did not move

---

[99]   Muslim, Hajj, 311; Ibn Sa'd, *Tabaqat*, 2:177; Maqrizi, *Imta al-Asma*, 7:240.

away from Allah's Messenger's door until morning, waiting, along with eminent members of Medina's tribes, without a wink of sleep. Meanwhile, the Messenger of Allah summoned Abu Bakr and Umar and consulted with them as to the kind of strategy they needed to pursue. He called for Bilal after the Morning Prayer. He wanted to follow the enemy, but was concerned that the hypocrites would use this situation to try to cover up their crimes. To prevent them from doing so, he ordered Bilal to call out through Medina's streets, "The Messenger of Allah commands you to seek out your enemy, and only those who participated in the battle yesterday shall go out."

Bilal used to continue his services as the Caller to Prayer in the best way during military expeditions also. Abu Juhayfa was one of those who could attest to this. The Companion relates an incident he witnessed:

"I happened to go the Messenger of Allah while he was at Abtah, in a red leather tent. It was midday and Bilal came out and recited the call to Prayer. I followed his mouth as he turned this side and that, as he said on the right and the left: "Come to the Prayer, come to salvation," and then he went back in. He came back out with the leftover ablution water of the Messenger of Allah. The people rushed to take some of it. Those who could, wiped their faces with it, while those who could not sought the blessings from the remaining water on their friends' hands.

Then Bilal went back inside and brought out a short staff, or spear (that was given to Allah's Messenger as a gift by the Abyssinian king). The Messenger of Allah followed, wearing a red mantle. It is as if I can still see the whiteness of his feet. Bilal fixed the spear for him in the ground (in front of the place where he would pray). He stepped forward to lead the noon Prayer, observing two units of Prayer. He then lead the afternoon Prayer. People and donkeys passed by in front of us as we prayed."[100]

ALWAYS READY FOR SERVICE

Bilal al-Habashi was at the Messenger's beckoning and call, day and night, during war and in peace, whenever and wherever they may be, was honored to serve, and sought any opportunity to be able to do even more. He once accompanied Allah's Messenger to the al-Baqi Cemetery. While walking through the graveyard, the Messenger of Allah said, "O Bilal, can

---

[100] Bukhari, Manaqib, 23; Muslim, Salat, 250; Bayhaqi, *Dala'il an-Nubuwwa*, 1:246.

you hear what I hear?" Bilal said, "No, by Allah, I cannot hear anything, O Messenger of Allah."

Allah's Messenger then said, "Can you not hear the punishment of the people of the grave?"[101]

The father of Abdullah at-Thaqafi relates another example:

"I participated in a military expedition with the Messenger of Allah. We were fasting as it was the month of Ramadan. When the time to the *iftar* (fast breaking dinner) approached, Bilal would come to us with food with which we could break our fast. We would ask, 'Has the Messenger of Allah eaten?' We did not want to eat without his having eaten first. Bilal would say, 'I did not come to you until the Messenger of Allah had eaten,' and that he would offer the food to Allah's Messenger first, who would put his hand in the dish and eat from it, after which we would follow. Bilal would also come to us with food for the pre-dawn meal."[102]

The Messenger of Allah sent a letter of invitation to Islam, to chief of the Banu Sahm, Ra'ya as-Sahmi, the latter then tearing the letter into shreds and hurled insults at Allah's Messenger. Allah's Messenger was very grieved upon learning of the situation, and thereupon sent a unit to the clan. When the clan's members got wind of the approach of the Muslim forces, they fled to higher ground. When the unit arrived in the region, there was no one to be seen. Surveying the area, they found a group in which members of the chief were also present. The unit took the group captive and returned to Medina.

When Ra'ya as-Sahmi heard what had happened, he flew into a rage. In his anger, he even forgot to change his clothes, mounting his horse and heading for Medina. He rode without break until he reached the village of his wife's relatives, the Banu Hilal. The men from the tribe were stunned to see him in his nightclothes, and immediately gave him something to wear. When he calmed down, they spoke with him and recommended that he become Muslim. But he rejected their advice, instead choosing to continue on his way. By the time he had reached Medina, night had already fallen. He waited for the morning. In the meantime, he thought about what the Banu Hilal had told him. The more he mused, the more he inclined to accepting Islam, and became free of the errors plaguing his mind and heart. After the Morning Prayer, he appeared before the Mes-

[101] *Musnad*, 3:151, 259; Shami, *Subul al-Huda*, 3:151, 259.
[102] Bayhaqi, *Dala'il an-Nubuwwa*, 5:305.

senger of Allah in remorse for all he had done. Ashamedly, he said, "O Messenger of Allah, give me your hand so that I may swear allegiance to you."

"Who are you?" Allah's Messenger asked.

"Ra'ya as-Sahm," he said quietly.

Pleased with the response he received, the Messenger of Allah held Ra'yat by the arm, raised it aloft, and, so as to prevent the people's treating him with hostility because of what he did, said, "O people, this is Ra'ya as-Sahmi who tore up the letter that I wrote to him and insulted me. He has felt remorse and repented for what he has done, and has embraced Islam." Ra'ya as-Sahmi then asked, "O Messenger of Allah, what will become of my children and wealth?" The Messenger of Allah said, "There is nothing I can do concerning your wealth, for it has been apportioned, but I can help in relation to your family. Go to the place where the captives are kept, determine their location, and come back to see me."

When Ra'ya went to where the captives were, he saw his son. He rushed back to Allah's Messenger.

"My son is a small way ahead, next to the Companions," he said. The Messenger of Allah addressed Bilal saying, "O Bilal, go with him and ask whether the child is indeed his. If the child recognizes his father, give him to his father."

Bilal rose immediately and took Ra'ya with him to see the child. With tears of joy, the father ran toward his son. Bilal asked the boy, "Is this your father?" The child said, "Yes," and threw his arms around his neck. Bilal watched in utter astonishment, as he had never seen such display of love towards children by the Arabs. He then handed the boy over to his father and returned to Allah's Messenger.

"O Messenger of Allah," he said. "Never have I seen one of the Arabs show such affection toward their child." Notably displeased with this attitude of the Arabs, Allah's Messenger said, "This is due to the Arabs' lack of affection."[103]

SECRETARY OF THE TREASURY

Exceptionally talented and dynamic, Bilal undertook several roles at the same time. Another one of critical posts Bilal held, in addition to being the

[103] Maqrizi, *Imta al-Asma*, 2:44.

Messenger's Caller to Prayer, and attending to his personal and official state duties, was the office of secretary of the treasury (*khazin al-bayt al-mal*). This was a function beyond just that of fiscal affairs. He would be responsible for the collection of the alms tax, charity, donations and spoils of war. Guarding them painstakingly, the Prophet's Companion would ensure that they were distributed to the necessary places in line with the commands of Allah's Messenger. One of the close witnesses of Bilal's service in this regard was Abdullah ibn Abbas. He relates:

"The Messenger of Allah went out one 'Eid morning and observed two units of Prayer. I did not see him observe such a Prayer nor before nor after it. He then went to the women with Bilal and addressed them, and he enjoined them to give in charity. So they began to give their rings, necklaces, and other things to Bilal, who was collecting them in the corner of his garment.[104]

Reporting this Tradition, Muhammad Hamidullah indicates that Bilal had undertaken the task of protecting all these items of jewelry that he had collected in alms and spending them in accordance with Allah's Messenger's directives.[105]

Sometimes Bilal would do this himself directly, while at other times, he would assist Allah's Messenger in this regard. On the return from Hunayn, the Muslim forces encamped at Ji'rana, near Mecca. The Messenger of Allah began distributing the war spoils, with Bilal's help. The hem of Bilal's garment was filled with the silver obtained in spoils. The Messenger of Allah took handfuls out of it and gave it to the people.

The abundance of war spoils at Ji'rana, when they were brought before the Messenger of Allah, left the people in sheer amazement. Astounded by what he saw, Abu Sufyan exclaimed, "O Messenger of Allah," he said. you have become the wealthiest of the Quraysh!" The Messenger of Allah merely smiled. Abu Sufyan said, "Would you give me from this wealth, O Messenger of Allah!"

The Messenger of Allah turned to Bilal, whom he had appointed to the task, and said, "O Bilal, measure for Abu Sufyan forty *uqiyya* of gold, and give him a hundred camels." Abu Sufyan said, "Give to my son, Yazid!" The Messenger of Allah said, "Measure for Yazid forty *uqiyya* of gold and give him a hundred camels." Having received what he wanted, Abu Sufyan

---

[104] Muslim, Salat al-Eidayn 13; Ibn Manzur, *Mukhtasar*, 22:344.
[105] Hamidullah, *The Life and Work of the Prophet of Islam*.

requested again, "Give to my son, Mu'awiya also, O Messenger of Allah." The Messenger of Allah said, "O Bilal, "Measure for him forty *uqiyya* of gold also and give him a hundred camels."

After the Battle of Hunayn, the Messenger of Allah gave the likes of Abu Sufyan and Safwan ibn Umayya a greater share of the spoils than Abbas ibn Mirdas. The fact that 'Abbas ibn Mirdas expressed this disparagingly in verse troubled Allah's Messenger, and he said,

"O Bilal, cut off this man's tongue."

Misunderstanding the Messenger's words, 'Abbas ibn Mirdas grew apprehensive when Bilal approached him.

"O Muslims," he called out, then pleading, "What are you doing? Would you cut off my tongue after I have become a Muslim? Please forgive me, O Messenger of Allah! I shall never utter such words again!" Seeing his apprehension, Bilal said, "Calm yourself! The Messenger of Allah commanded me not to cut off your tongue, but merely to silence you with some food and some clothing!"

Bilal al-Habashi had many precious moments while fulfilling his mission, and was favored with a great many blessings. Abu Musa relates what happened in the aftermath of the Battle of Hunayn:

"I was in the company of the Messenger of Allah as he encamped in Ji'rana (a place) between Mecca and Medina and Bilal was also there.

There came to Allah's Messenger a Bedouin, and he said, 'Muhammad, fulfill what you have promised me.' The Messenger of Allah said to him, 'I can convey to you glad tidings.' (Oblivious to the worth of such tidings) the Bedouin said, 'Give me more than just glad tidings.' Then the Messenger of Allah turned to me (i.e., Abu Musa) and Bilal, and said,

'This man has rejected glad tidings, but would you two accept them?' Bilal and I exclaimed, 'Of course we accept them, O Messenger of Allah!' Then Allah's Messenger asked for a bowl of water and washed both his hands and face in it. He then took a mouthful of water, spurted it back into the container, and said to us, 'Now, you two drink of it and pour the rest over your faces and necks.' We took the drinking bowl and did as Allah's Messenger had instructed us to do. Umm Salama then called out from behind a screen, 'Spare some for your mother,' so we left some of for her."[106]

---

[106] Bukhari, Maghazi, 56; Muslim, Fada'il as-Sahaba, 164; Abu Ya'la, *Musnad*, 7277; Dhahabi, *Siyar A'lam an-Nubala*, 3334.

Diligently completing all the tasks given him, Bilal would strive to fulfil them in the best possible way. Harith ibn Yazid relates: "The Messenger of Allah sent Mu'adh ibn Jabal to the people of Himyar, Amr ibn Sulaym to the people of Kinda and Hadramawt, and 'Awf ibn Malik to the people of Najran. Companions informed of the matter used to say, 'The Messenger of Allah commanded us to give to Bilal al-Habashi the alms tax levied on fruit and vegetables, and he appointed Bilal with the collection and protection of the prescribed alms.'"[107]

STATE EXPENDITURE

Bilal would buy and sell, on behalf of the Messenger of Allah and the state, borrow money, and fulfill the requirements of contracted agreements. Jabir ibn Abdullah reports that he was once in the company of the Messenger of Allah, travelling from Mecca to Medina on his camel which had grown jaded. Noticing the situation, the Messenger of Allah overtook him, and after conversing with him for a while, he said, "Sell me this camel of yours, O Jabir."

Jabir said, "It is yours."

Allah's Messenger said, "No, sell it to me."

"But it is yours, O Messenger of Allah," Jabir said.

The Messenger of Allah said again, "Sell it to me," to which Jabir replied, "Then give me an *uqiyya* of gold, for I owe that to a person, and then it would be yours."

The Messenger of Allah said, "I have bought it from you, and you can repay your debt when you reach Medina." When I reached Medina, the Messenger of Allah said to Bilal,

"Give him an *uqiyya* of gold and make some extra payment too."

Bilal did just as he had been commanded to do, giving Jabir me an *uqiyya* of gold and a fraction more.[108]

Bilal served under the supervision of Allah's Messenger, and when he made a mistake, was exhorted to the correct action or conduct. For this reason, even though he worried about erring, he was nonetheless at ease because of his knowing that he would be guided in the event that he had. Years down the track, Bilal related that he once had a quantity of dates

[107] Baladhuri, *Ansab al-Ashraf*, 1:621.
[108] Muslim, Musaqa, 111.

belong to Allah's Messenger. When he realized that they had begun to spoil, he took them to the market so that they would not be wasted, whereby he exchanged two volumes of inferior quality dates for one volume of higher quality. When he took the newly purchased dates as food for Allah's Messenger, the Messenger inquired about their source. Bilal explained what he had done, to which the Messenger of Allah responded, "This is precisely the forbidden usury! Do not do this! Go at once and return them. Sell those of inferior quality in exchange for silver, gold, or wheat, and the use the proceeds to buy the other."[109]

Bilal was extremely dependable, had an advanced degree of competence and superior social skills, and successfully carried out all the service he performed. He oversaw the running of the yet unnamed fiscal institution of the Muslim state with great success for years on end, in line with the commands of Allah's Messenger.

MARRIAGE

Bilal's enslavement during his youth meant that he was not able to marry, while his struggle in the call and service to Islam prevented his marriage later on. He put off marriage for a long period of time due to his intensive activities. The Messenger of Allah who knew him closely helped him enter into marriage when the opportunity arose.

A few members of the Banu Bukayr once came to visit the Messenger of Allah. They stated that they wanted to marry off their daughter Hind and appealed to him for help in finding her a suitable spouse. After listening to them, Allah's Messenger said, "Where do you stand in relation to Bilal (indicating that they should consider Bilal as a potential husband)?"

They did not wish to give their daughter in marriage to a freed slave, but they did not want to refuse Allah's Messenger either. So they merely returned without responding to his counsel. Some time later, they came a second time and repeated their request from the first meeting. The Messenger of Allah said again, "Where do you stand in relation to Bilal?" Again, they did not answer, instead seeking the Messenger's leave. When they returned a third time, the Messenger of Allah said, "Where do you stand in relation to a man who is one of the people of Paradise?" He thus indicated that he could not make sense of their reluctance. Mellowing out

---

[109] *Musnad*, 2:21; Abu Ya'la, *Musnad*, 5684; Tabarani, *Al-Mu'jam al-Kabir*, 1:339.

with the insistence of Allah's Messenger, the Banu Bukayr members then agreed and gave their daughter in marriage to Bilal al-Habashi.[110]

Clearly, that the Banu Bukayr were as yet unable to interiorize the truth that goodness and righteousness was not based on blood or lineage, but came with piety and God-consciousness. Of course it was not at all easy for an attitude that had settled for centuries to be uprooted in such a short period of time. Even if somethings are accepted rationally, old understandings are not so easily abandoned, and the truth submitted to.

What her family proved unable to overcome, the bride had long prevailed over. Upon becoming informed of the matter, she was most upset and disappointed by her family's attitude. Rejoicing at the prospect of marriage with the Messenger's recommendation, the young woman intervened to tell her family that what they had done was a mistake, and that they needed to rectify it immediately.

Bilal himself explains that when he went to meet Hind's family, he faced the resistance of her brothers. He did not respond, to prevent matters from getting worse, going instead to Allah's Messenger for advice.

Bilal told the Messenger of Allah how offended he was by the treatment of the Banu Bukayr and their efforts to impede the marriage.

Allah's Messenger was angered by what he heard and took action immediately, sending word to the Banu Bukayr and summoning them to his presence. Upon learning of the Messenger's call, they knew that it concerned the marriage and thus became apprehensive, scolding their sister as a result.

"Look at what has befallen us because of you!" they snapped. This was the manner in which Hind became aware of her family's attitude, and she retorted, "How can you prevent my marrying Bilal al-Habashi despite the recommendation of Allah's Messenger?" She then added, "I give full power to the Messenger of Allah, and will marry whomsoever he wishes me to marry."

Realizing their mistake, the Banu Bukayr went to Allah's Messenger and apologized for their actions. They then began preparations for Hind's marriage to Bilal.[111]

---

[110] Ibn Sa'd, *Tabaqat*, 3:237.
[111] Qurtubi, *Al-Jami' li Ahkam al-Qur'an*, 8:610; Ibn Manzur, *Mukhtasar*, 27:296.

MARRIAGE IMBUED WITH THE PROPHETIC CULTIVATION

The marriage of Bilal al-Habashi and Hind was a happy one. The only issue proved to be Bilal's relating at length everything he experienced with and heard from Allah's Messenger when he went home. The Companion constantly in the company of Allah's Messenger and serving him, was devoted to him with great sincerity. He would listen to him very carefully, inscribing his words on to his heart, and put them into practice at the very first opportunity. As he wanted his wife to be acquainted with and practice these also, the first thing he did when he got home would be to tell his wife everything he heard from Allah's Messenger with great enthusiasm. His sincerity, diligence and excitement preventing his seeing the effect this had on his wife, the latter entertaining certain doubts and supposing him to have exaggerated in his reports. At times, the issue grew enough as to cause contention between them. On one such occasion, the Messenger of Allah called upon them in their home. Bilal's wife narrates the rest:

"The Messenger of Allah once came to our house, and after offering his greeting asked if Bilal was at home. It was one of the days that I was vexed by what Bilal had said, and my vexation projected onto to my manner. 'No," I replied coldly.

Noticing the tone in my voice, the Messenger of Allah said, 'It seems you are angry with Bilal.'

'Indeed, I am,' I began, expressing my concerns as to the authenticity of his reports. 'When he comes home after having left you, he often says, 'The Messenger of Allah said this, the Messenger of Allah did that.' The Messenger of Allah then said, 'All that Bilal transmits from me is truth. Bilal would never speak a word otherwise.' He then cautioned, 'Be not angry with Bilal. Do not forget that your deeds will not be acceptable so long as you remain angry with him.'"[112]

This experience enabled both of them to see the truth and set right their mistakes. Listening to a great many Traditions from him, his wife Hind al-Khawlani used to say that her husband constantly made the following supplication:

---

[112] Ibn Hisham, *Sira*, 11869; Ibn al-Athir, *Usd al-Ghaba*, 7338.

"My Lord, accept from me my deeds of righteousness, forgive me my errors and sins, and excuse my mistakes."

SECOND MARRIAGE

The years passed, and after the demise of Allah's Messenger, Bilal al-Habashi could not bear to stay in Medina, settling instead in Damascus. It was here that his beloved wife passed away. Bilal was deeply grieved by her passing. Some time later, upon the encouragement of his brother in faith Abu Ruwayha of Khatham, he decided to marry again. Together, in Damascus, they sought to marry daughters of the Banu Layth, and married once they were accepted as suitors.[113]

Abu Darda, who witnessed their marriage, relates: "Some time after Bilal al-Habashi's settling in Damascus, he and the Companion the Messenger of Allah declared to be his brother sought to marry women from the same clan. He said to their family: 'I am Bilal and this is my brother. We were astray and Allah guided us. We were enslaved and Allah freed us. We were impoverished and Allah gave us wealth. If you should consent to our marrying your daughters, all praise is due to Allah; and if you should turn us away, there is no strength or power save with Allah.'

The household accepted their offer of marriage and united each of them in wedlock with a suitable partner from their tribe.[114]

[113] Ibn Manzur, *Mukhtasar*, 1:304.
[114] Ibn al-Athir, *Usd al-Ghaba*, 493.

CHAPTER 4

AFTER THE MESSENGER

When the Companions heard of Allah's Messenger's demise in Medina, they did not want to believe it for a long time. When they confronted the truth, some stood aghast, and some were completely dumbfounded. Their tears did not stop. Like the others, Bilal too wept unceasingly, the tears flowing down his face moistening his beard. But the tears would not abate, even if days, weeks, and months went by.

Jabir ibn Abdullah narrates:

"I once saw Bilal ibn Rabah beside the grave of the Messenger of Allah. He was sprinkling water over the grave of Allah's Messenger, from a waterskin. Starting from the head section of the grave, he sprinkled his way to the feet."[115]

Separation from the Messenger was very difficult for someone who never left his side, even during military expeditions. Everything reminded him of Allah's Messenger, and he saw him wherever he looked, his memories coming to life before his very eyes. The world in all its expanse seemed to him so narrow, like the walls were caving in on him. He was no longer to wander through the streets. He just wanted to get out of Medina, get away as soon as he possibly could. He went to Abu Bakr to inform him of this request.

The caliph could not find it in his heart to let the Messenger's Caller to Prayer leave the city, and upon his insistence, Bilal stayed. Life in Medina, however, proved very difficult for him. At each and every call to Prayer the words lodged in his throat and he just could not get them out. He shed tears copiously. When Abu Bakr passed away, Bilal went to Umar to repeat his request. Umar did not want him to leave Medina either. He only consented upon Bilal's vigorous insistence. Bilal left Medina to carry Allah's Name to all corners of the world, to strive in His way.

Settling in Damascus after Abu Bakr's death, Bilal stayed here for eight years, until his own death, on the twentieth year of Emigration.

As soon as he left Medina, he went straight to the frontline, joining the forces of Abu Ubayda ibn al-Jarrah, which continued its march to Emesa (Hims) after Damascus. In the winter of the sixteenth year after the emigration, Abu Ubayda ibn al-Jarrah laid siege to the city alongside Khalid ibn al-Walid. Showing incredible fortitude in the face of freezing cold

---

[115] Bayhaqi, *Dala'il an-Nubuwwa*, 7:264.

temperatures, the Muslim forces continue the siege against all the odds. Their patience was instrumental in drawing Allah's mercy. While the Byzantine troops suffered frostbite and frozen feet despite their heavy leather boots, the Muslim soldiers were not exposed to such troubles despite wearing on their feet but sandals.

An extraordinary event took place during the siege. One morning, a group of Companions including Bilal al-Habashi, Miqdad ibn Amr, and Abdullah ibn Mas'ud began collectively proclaiming Allah's greatness, the reverberating sound shaking the thick fort walls. So loudly had they raised the phrase "Allah is the All-Great" that the city's inhabitants, in their terror, could not understand what was happening. When the Companions raised the cry a second time, the fort shook once again and the walls of people's houses cracked. At the third cry, the walls of the fort cracked. Terrified and panic-stricken, the people ran to the city's elders, crying out, "Do you not see what has befallen us and the situation we are in? What (more) are you waiting for? If you do not act fast, everything will be destroyed, and nothing shall remain standing!"

The governors took heed of the people's words and sent word to the Muslims that they wished to make a truce. After consulting with the commanders, Abu Ubayda concluded an agreement on the terms of the peace agreement negotiated in Damascus.

Bilal al-Habashi, fought on the frontline until his death in Damascus on the twentieth year of Emigration, accompanied Abu Ubayda ibn al-Jarrah and Khalid ibn al-Walid during the Damascus conquest. Both commanders devoted close attention to him and did not neglect asking his opinion. Salih ibn Kaysan relates: "Umar was informed in writing of bad management on the part of commander Khalid ibn al-Walid, in regard to the appropriation of funds from the state treasury. To ascertain the accuracy of the information, he wrote a letter to Commander-in-Chief Abu Ubayda ibn al-Jarrah. In the letter, he instructed: 'Ask Khalid (concerning this matter)... If he confesses to having used the spoils, he is guilty of misappropriation. If he claims to have given from his own pocket, he is guilty of extravagance. In either case dismiss him, and take charge of his duties. Once you have dismissed him from his post, divide his wealth and appoint whomsoever you wish in his stead.'

Having read the letter, Abu Ubayda postponed taking action for some time, instead of acting upon it immediately, so as not to demoralize the troops. Abu Ubayda, himself a great admirer of Khalid ibn al-Walid's service, withheld the letter until the conquest of Damascus, and made no mention of it to anybody.

Bilal al-Habashi, however, was aware of the situation and went straight to Abu Ubayda.

'What has Umar written to you about concerning Khalid,' he asked.

'He has instructed me to investigate the accusations that have been leveled against Khalid. He says that if he concedes guilt, dismiss him from his post; if he does not, then he may continue in his post.' He advised, 'It is not befitting that you delay carrying out the orders of the Commander of the Believers. You must fulfil his command immediately.' Seeing the Companion as justified in his words, Abu Ubayda related the situation to Khalid ibn al-Walid. Khalid ibn al-Walid requested time to consult his sister, and Abu Ubayda agreed to wait. Khalid then went to see his sister, whose opinion he valued highly, to seek her advice on the matter. For he trusted her word as much as not to object to almost anything she said. When he put the issue to her, she was somewhat emotional: 'By Allah,' she said, 'Umar seeks to dismiss you, and he wants that you should confess to some oversight that he may indeed dismiss you.'

'You are right,' Khalid said, thereby kissing his sister on the forehead and returning to Abu Ubayda.

Khalid thus resigned from office, handing over the necessary property to the Commander-in-Chief, under Bilal al-Habashi's supervision."[116]

Bilal al-Habashi oversaw financial affairs after the Messenger's demise, just as he had during his lifetime, and he openly expressed his views and individual judgments in this regard to the caliphs. After the conquest of such places as Damascus, Jazira, Kufa, Basra, and Fustat during Umar's caliphate, differing views were put forward in relation to the division of the lands. Umar avoiding distributing to the troops directly, commanding instead that they be left to the people and that they, in turn, be subject to the *kharaj* tax, imposed on lands conquered militarily. Many Companions opposed his view, the toughest opposition coming from Zubayr ibn al-Awwam and Bilal al-Habashi.[117]

Umar held Bilal al-Habashi in high esteem, taking his objections seriously and trying his utmost not to offend him. He would even specifically

---

[116] Ibn Manzur, *Mukhtasar*, 8:23.
[117] *Doğuştan Günümüze Büyük İslâm Tarihi*, 2:227.

instruct and exhort those he authorized to look out for those Companions like Suhayb and Bilal al-Habashi.[118]

When he arrived in Damascus and was to visit and review its administrators he took alongside him the highly trusted Bilal al-Habashi. Together they first went to the house of Abu Ubayda and then Khalid ibn al-Walid. When they reached the latter's home, Bilal sought permission to enter. The door was opened and they were welcomed. When they entered, Khalid ibn al-Walid was busy with his arrow. When Umar saw a chest in his home, he opened it, supposing it to have been filled with silver or gold coins, but he was mistaken. In the chest was only a single coat of mail. Umar was pleased at his having thus been mistaken and with what he saw, leaving the house after a some discussion. From there they went to the home of Amr ibn al-As.[119]

Once inspections were complete, Umar gathered together all the commanders and consulted with them on various issues. Bilal al-Habashi, who learned of the meeting, went to take part. Addressing the gathering at one point, he exhorted Umar in the matter of the difficulties faced by the common folk and the extravagance of the leaders.

"O Umar," he began.

"You stand between these commanders and Allah, but there is no one standing between you and Allah. Take a look at the men standing in front of you, to your right and to your left. By Allah, these men eat only the flesh of fowl."

"You are right," said Umar, then turning to the commanders and saying, "O Commanders, by Allah I will not leave until you I receive from each of you the guarantee that you will provide the Muslims with at least two (*mudd*)[120] measures of wheat and olive oil and vinegar to go with it, at the beginning of each month." Accepting his order, the commanders said, "O Commander of the Believers, we consider this as binding on us. Moreover, Allah has bestowed abundant blessing upon the Muslims, and we shall not find it difficult to fulfil your command." Satisfied with the answer he received, Umar said, "So it is settled," and thus reassured Bilal.[121]

---

[118] Maqdisi, *Ansab al-Qurashiyyin*, 474.

[119] Mustafa Fayda, *Allah'ın Kılıcı*, 446.

[120] *Mudd*: a dry measure equivalent to 832 grams.

[121] Ibn al-Athir, *Al-Kamil fi at-Tarikh*, 2:562.

Upon seeing client of Umar Zayd ibn Aslam to be dispirited during the Caliph's visit to Syria, Bilal approached him and asked, "O Aslam, How do you find Umar?"

Aslam said, "The best of people, except that when he becomes angry it is a mighty matter." Bilal said, "If I was with him when he became angry, I would recite the Qur'an to him until his anger subsided." Following Bilal's advice, Aslam was able to better deal with such situations.

HIS DEATH

Emigrating to Damascus during the caliphate of Umar, Bilal al-Habashi lived here until his death in the eighteenth or twentieth year of emigration, when, by now in his mid-sixties, he took ill. Those who heard of his death were devastated. They washed and enshrouded him in tears, burying him in Bab as-Saghir cemetery after observing his Funeral Prayer. He was not known to have any children.[122]

Bilal possessed an unceasingly belief, love for Allah and His Messenger, and zeal. Realizing that he was about to breathe his last on his deathbed, his wife cried out, "Woe is me!" Bilal injected saying, "Now is not the time for sorrow. It is the time for joy and jubilation, for tomorrow I shall meet the beloved Muhammad and his Companions!"[123]

Bilal al-Habashi for years endured the most unbearable of suffering for the sake of his belief. It is on account of this that he was time after time declared one of those promised Paradise, by the beloved Messenger. He was one of the Messenger's greatest devotees. Medina had become much too constricted for him following the demise of Allah's Messenger. He spent the remainder of his life on the battlefield, as though trying to forget the pain of separation. Now was the time for joy for Bilal al-Habashi.

As he lay on his deathbed, his loved ones stood around him shedding tears of sadness at the time for separation. But Bilal took no heed. As he smiled with great happiness and savored the insatiable taste of reunion, he said to those around him, "Tomorrow I will meet my friends, Muhammad and his blessed party."

The long and arduous journey had now come to an end, and he had reunited with his beloved. For, death was a reunion for those happy souls

---

[122] Ibn Abd al-Barr, *Isti'ab*, 1:178; Ibn Sa'd, *Tabaqat*, 3:238; Ibn al-Jawzi, *Sifat as-Safwa*, 24.
[123] Zarqani, *Sharh al-Mawahib*, 1:499.

who saw the Age of Happiness. It was a return to the true homeland, the point at which separation ended. Bilal al-Habashi mixed at his last breath the pangs of death with the honey of reunion, and kneaded, until finally tasting of it with love.

Peace be upon those heroes of service who, by taking his example, break the chains of their ego and carnal desires, who liberate their spirit with belief, and who dedicate themselves to Islam.

May Allah be well pleased with him.